QUICK AND EASY
WOODEN
TOYS

QUICK AND EASY
WOODEN TOYS

ALAN PINDER

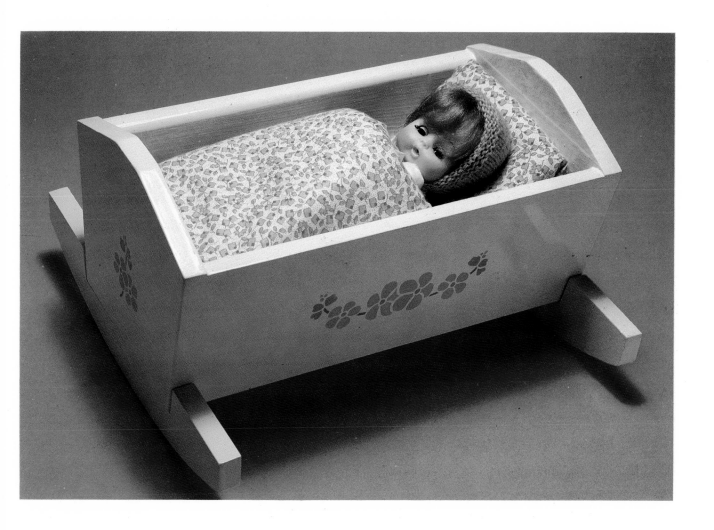

SEARCH PRESS

Pitman

Melbourne London Toronto Boston Wellington

First published in Great Britain 1986

by SEARCH PRESS LTD.,
Wellwood, North Farm Road
Tunbridge Wells, Kent. TN2 3DR

First published in Australia 1986

by Pitman Publishing Pty Ltd
(Incorporated in Victoria)
Kings Gardens
95 Coventry Street
South Melbourne
Victoria 3205

41 Albion Street
Surrey Hills
New South Wales 2010

Unit 17
Paddington Market
261–265 Given Terrace
Paddington
Queensland 4064

Associated Companies

Pitman Publishing Ltd
London

Copp Clark Pitman
Toronto

Pitman Publishing New Zealand Ltd
Wellington

National Library of Australia
Cataloguing in Publication data

Pinder, Alan
    Quick and Easy Wooden Toys
Includes index
ISBN 7299 0001 0
    1. Wooden toy making.   I. Title

The author and publishers would like to thank Messrs Whites Bazaar of
Monson Road, Tunbridge Wells for help in providing the models in the
photograph of the castle. The author would also like to acknowledge the
invaluable experience and advice of Les Bartle.

ISBN   (UK) 0 85532 561 5
ISBN (AUS) 0 7299 0001 0

Printed in Spain by Elkar S. Coop, Bilbao 12

CONTENTS

AUTHOR'S NOTE

For each of the toys described in this book I have provided diagrams, to show the stages of making, and exploded drawings. The latter show the materials and the measurements needed for each component. The components are numbered, and are referred to throughout the main text in brackets, as (1) etc.

INTRODUCTION

The intention of this book is to show how simple wooden toys can be made quickly and cheaply without the aid of an expensive workshop and by using only wooden fittings.

Obviously a certain number of basic hand tools are required, but most households will possess them. If, however, you possess also a few power tools, these will help you considerably.

An uncle of mine, who was a carpenter, used to make many beautiful pieces of furniture. He also made toys for me, for my brother and various of my cousins. When, as a child, I watched him at work in his workshop, he used to say to me, "I never throw any wood away, you never know when it will do for something". As he said this, he would be neatly stacking away little offcuts of wood. I have always done the same and, consequently, most of the wood I use has been stored in the cellar for some while, and this helps to keep cost down considerably. If you do not have a cellarful of bits and pieces of wood, the cost of buying wood from a DIY shop is still reasonable compared to the cost of buying a finished toy in a shop.

I always prefer to use a suitable piece of hardwood, but if none of this type of wood is available then any softwood will suit almost as well.

When I was making the toys in this book, I worked to measurements in inches, and these are the figures I have given with each set of instructions. I have provided, in addition, the equivalent metric measurements which I have computed to the nearest millimetre. Any of the toys can, however, be adapted to suit your own ideas or requirements, or even the size of the piece of wood you are working. When my children were of playschool age I used to make several toys for their playroom, including a playhouse, painting easels, and a table and benches. In summer, when the sun shone, the children would take the table and benches out into the garden and have all their meals there.

When the children outgrew the playroom, I dismantled the easels and the playhouse and, from the same pieces of wood, I made them a bookcase for their school books to be kept in, which they still use today.

All the toys and games I describe are very robust and should easily stand up to the rigours of life with children.

To enable the reader to follow, and copy, my method I have given with each toy an exploded drawing in which the parts are numbered and listed. Also at the beginning of the book I have described in words and drawings the tools needed to make 'Quick and Easy Wooden Toys'.

Working surfaces

The first piece of equipment you need to work on is a rigid flat surface which will support the wood whilst you are working with it.

A purpose-made work-bench is ideal. This is expensive but a worthwhile investment. Usually, a work-bench has a woodworker's vice permanently fixed to the work-top, near to a leg for extra strength. The woodworker's vice has powerful jaws lined with wood to prevent any damage to the work being held in the vice.

As an alternative, portable work-benches can be purchased. These are self-standing, and the work-top operates as a long vice. Because of the length of the jaws, irregular shapes of timber can be gripped.

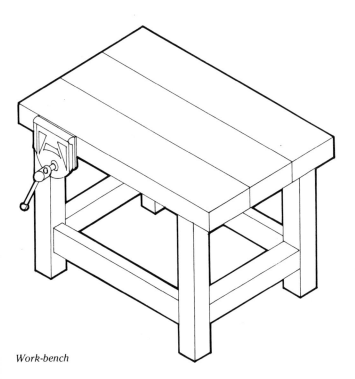

Work-bench

Portable work-bench

Basic hand-tools

MARKING OUT TOOLS

Metal combination, or mitre, square. Also known as Adjustable Try. This is a popular and robust tool for marking out 45-degree and 90-degree angles.

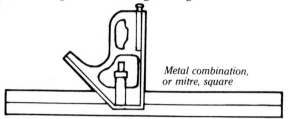

Metal combination, or mitre, square

The adjustable metal stock allows for the checking of external and internal right angles. When using the combination square always check that the locking nut is tightened for accurate marking.

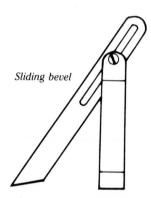

Sliding bevel

Sliding bevel. A useful tool which has a movable blade for marking unusual angles.

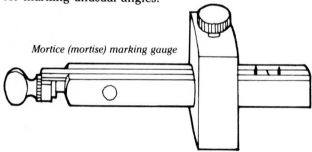

Mortice (mortise) marking gauge

Marking gauge. This gauge is used for marking out mortice and tenon joints. It has two points, which are adjustable to the width required and mark parallel lines on the wood. The width of a mortice (mortise) should not exceed one third of the thickness of the wood.

This gauge is similar to a basic marking gauge which has only one point, but many gauges are now manufactured combining both types.

See diagram.

SAWS

There are a number of different saws available and each has a specific job to do. Each saw blade varies in the number and size of teeth it possesses. Teeth or 'points' are measured by the inch (1in = 25mm). The greater number of teeth per inch, the finer the cut.

The following are the types of saw used in making the toys in this book:

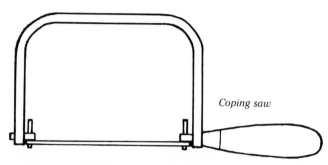

Coping saw

Coping saw. This is the best all-round saw for curved and specially shaped work, and it is adequate for all the shapes required in this book.

The saw will cut any shape but can only saw as far into the piece of wood as the distance between the blade and the top of the frame will allow.

The blades have very fine teeth and are fitted into clips at each side of the frame. When these are blunt they can be replaced.

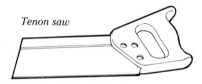

Tenon saw

Tenon saw. The tenon saw is a fine-toothed saw with 14-16 teeth per inch, and it has a heavy steel or brass back. This gives rigidity to the blade for accurate cutting of fine work. As the name implies it is used for cutting tenon joints (see page 15). It can also be used for cutting most other joints.

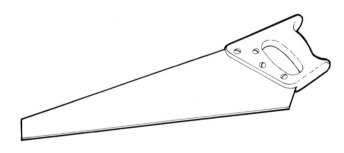

Ripsaw. The ripsaw has large teeth, 4 per inch (25mm) and is used for cutting timber along the grain. This it does very quickly.

Crosscut saw. The crosscut saw, as its name suggests, is used for cutting across the grain of thick timber. It has slightly smaller teeth than that of a ripsaw, but it still leaves a rough cut.

Panel saw. The panel saw is the most versatile of handsaws, and, unless you intend to do a lot of heavy work, it is the principal handsaw you will use. The teeth are smaller than on the crosscut saw and this gives a smoother cut.

PLANES

The basic job of a plane is to clean and reduce wood in dimension, leaving it smooth and flat. This is done by a cutting blade fixed in the body of the plane.

As with saws, there are a number of different planes available.

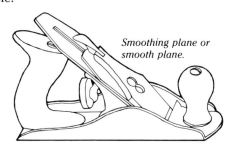

Smoothing plane or smooth plane.

Smoothing plane. The smoothing plane is 8in-10in long (200mm-250mm) and it is the most popular type of metal-bench plane. It can be used for final finishing, leaving the wood smooth and flat, but it can also be used for heavier general woodwork.

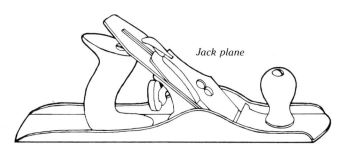

Jack plane

Jack plane. This is longer than a smoothing plane — 14in-15in long (350mm-375mm). This longer base enables a flatter surface to be cut on longer pieces of wood.

For sharpening plane blades, see uncut Oilstone.

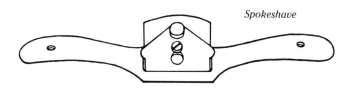

Spokeshave

SPOKESHAVE

There are two patterns of spokeshave, which is a tool used to shape curved surfaces. One pattern has a flat surface for use on concave curves. They give as fine a finish as a plane. When you use a spokeshave, always work with the grain of the wood.

CLAW HAMMERS

The only hammer you require is a claw hammer, preferably of 16oz (454g). This is the weight of the head. The claw can be used to pull out most types of nail. For striking a chisel which has a wooden handle, use a joiner's mallet.

CHISELS

Chisels are used for removing areas of wood to receive hinges or other fittings, or for removing wood for jointing purposes.

The only type of chisel you require is:

Bevel-edge chisel. This chisel will perform all the chiselling jobs required for these toys. As the name suggests, it has a bevel edge and can reach into awkward corners.

Four sizes of chisel — ¼in, ½in, ¾in and 1in (6mm, 12mm, 18mm and 25mm, respectively) will suffice. Many chisels manufactured today have shockproof and splinterproof plastic handles which can be struck with a metal-headed hammer. If you have the traditional boxwood or beech-handled chisels, then these must be hit with a joiner's mallet, otherwise they will splinter.

For sharpening chisels, I recommend the use of a homing guide. See under Oilstone (page 11).

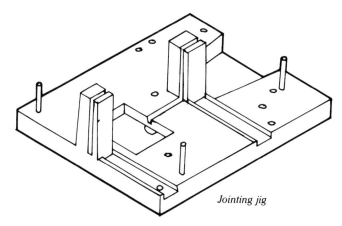

Jointing jig

MULTI-PURPOSE JOINTING JIG

This tool has two guides into which the saw is placed. It is then drawn backwards and forwards to cut the wood vertically. The base of the jig has holes into which plastic pegs are inserted. These can be set at various angles for whatever cut is required.

The jointing jig can also be used for cutting out more complicated joints. None of these, however, is required for the toys in this book.

CRAMP, OR CLAMP, TOOLS

Clamps, or cramps, are essential for holding pieces of wood while you are marking, sawing, drilling, or glueing them together.

The two main types are:

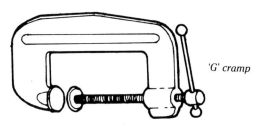

'G' cramp

'G' Cramps. These are the most useful. They are light in weight and easily portable. They are available in various sizes with openings up to 8in (200mm) wide.

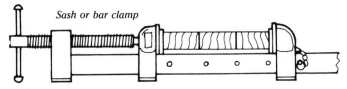

Sash or bar clamp

Sash, or bar, clamps hold large pieces of work together together while they are being glued. They consist of two adjustable shoes on a long metal bar of up to 6 feet (180cm) in length. One shoe slides along the bar, and is secured with a metal pin. The other shoe is tightened to the work by a screw.

With both types of cramp, it is advisable to use two at a time so that even pressure can be applied on the whole surface of the work. However, do not over-tighten them with a spanner as this will distort the cramp. Also place scrap pieces of wood between the cramp and the work in order that damage to the edges or surface of the wood is prevented.

HAND DRILL

The hand drill, used with twist drills, is employed to bore holes in wood up to ¼in (6mm) diameter, slowly but accurately. The hand drill has a chuck which will only accommodate round-shanked drills.

Brace

BRACE

A swing brace, used with bits, bores holes up to 1in (25mm) diameter accurately in wood. The brace has a chuck with jaws, which will accept square-ended bits securely.

Twist drill

TWIST DRILL

Twist drills are available in sizes up to ½in (12mm) for use with a hand drill or power drill, but do not use a hand drill above the ¼in (6mm) size. The drills have round shanks.

Twist bit

TWIST BIT

There are many types of bit, but the most accurate and efficient is called a "Jennings" or double-twist auger bit. This leaves a smooth, clean-cut hole. Twist bits have a square end which, when clamped in the chuck of the brace, will not slip when the holes are being bored.

To avoid splitting the wood when boring with a twist bit proceed as follows: bore the hole until the tip of the bit just breaks through the other side of the wood. Remove the bit and turn the piece of wood around. Resume boring from this side with the tip of the bit being placed in the hole it made from the other side. By doing this the hole will have clean-cut edges.

If it is not possible to bore from both sides, place a scrap piece of wood behind the hole and let the bit bore into this. This prevents the wood splitting.

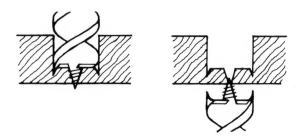

COUNTERSINK BIT

A countersink bit is used with a hand-drill or brace to form a recess in the top of a hole to allow the countersink screwhead to finish flush with the surface of the wood.

Countersink bit

SCREWDRIVERS

Screwdrivers are probably the commonest tool in any household, but it is important to use the correct one for the job.

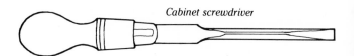

Cabinet screwdriver

Cabinet screwdriver. This is the most common type available. It has an oval shaped wooden boxwood handle which gives maximum grip, and is adequate to deal with any screws involved in making these toys.

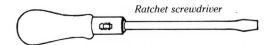

Ratchet screwdriver

Ratchet screwdriver. This possesses a reversible ratchet which cuts out the need to change grip continually as you turn the handle. All screwdriver tips should be flat in order to fit correctly into the head of the screw. They should not overlap the slot in the screw head, as this will

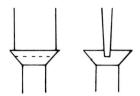

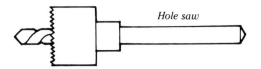

Hole saw

damage the wood as the screw head enters it. When you use screwdrivers, keep the end of the blade squarely in the screw slot to avoid damaging the screw head.

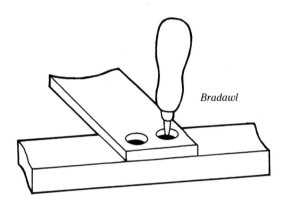

Bradawl

BRADAWL

The bradawl is an inexpensive tool useful for starting screw holes in wood and preventing the wood from splitting.

Bradawls have either a square section or round section point. The square section type is easier for penetrating the wood. After twisting in the wood, it is easily pulled out.

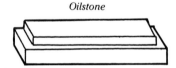

Oilstone

OILSTONE or BENCH STONE

An oilstone or bench stone (also known as slipstone) is essential for sharpening plane blades and chisels. It is very difficult to obtain a good result with blunt tools.

Oilstones are usually two-sided. One side has a medium grit surface and the other a fine one. The medium side is for removing small chips in the cutting blades, and the fine side is for putting the final cutting edge to a blade.

For sharpening plane blades and chisels, I recommend using also a *homing guide*. Plane blades and chisels are clamped in the jaws of the homing guide and rubbed up and down the oilstone. The homing guide will give you the correct angle for each blade and keep it constant whilst sharpening is in progress.

HOLE SAW

You will not find this in a basic tool kit. The hole saw is only required if you intend to make your own wheels, as I did.

The hole saw, which can be used in a brace or an electric drill with a low speed, consists of a saw blade moulded into a circle. This fits into a circular metal base through

the centre of which passes a ⅜in (9mm) centre pivot drill These can be purchased with multiple saw blades. A hole saw is ideal for cutting wheels as the drill makes a hole for the axle to pass through in the centre of the disc.

POWER TOOLS

With the addition of power tools to a workshop, many of the tedious and arduous tasks can be completed more easily and accurately.

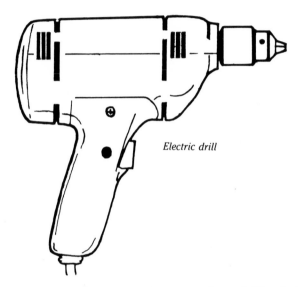

Electric drill

Electric drill. An electric drill, apart from drilling holes, can be converted to many other tools with the addition of different attachments, e.g. circular saw, sanding discs.

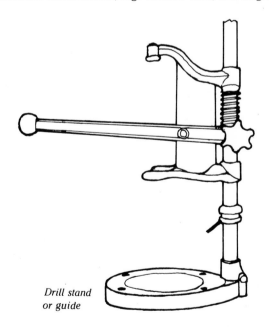

Drill stand or guide

Drill stand. The drill stand (or guide) holds the electric drill vertical and ensures accurate drilling at right angles to a piece of wood.

The drill bit is lowered into the wood by means of a lever arm. If you buy the drill stand and electric drill separately, make sure that the drill will fit the stand!

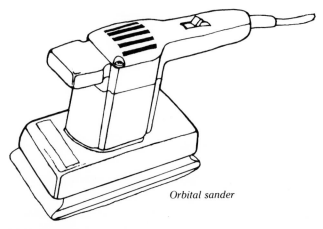

Orbital sander

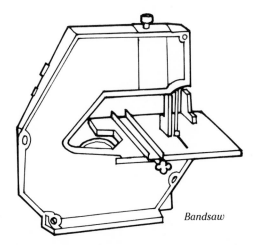

Bandsaw

Bandsaw. A bandsaw, as the name suggests, is a continuous band of metal with saw teeth cut in it, fitted over two or three wheels and stretched tight.

The wheels rotate the metal band which will cut curves quickly and accurately. It also cuts in straight lines with the aid of guides.

Bandsaws are now manufactured in small compact units which will fit easily on to a bench top; and they will eliminate a lot of tedious sawing of curves with a coping saw.

Orbital sander. An orbital sander has a flat rubber surface over which the abrasive sanding paper is stretched. The flat surface then rotates in very small circles to give a fine smooth finish to the wood. This type of sander, which will save you much physical work, can be purchased as a tool, or as an attachment for use with an electric drill.

Wood: important hints

There are two categories of wood — softwood and hardwood. Softwood, as its name implies, is easily worked, and therefore ideal for making simple wooden toys.

Hardwoods are more expensive, but they are also more generally resistant to surface marking and, for outside use, have a longer life than softwoods.

The way to distinguish softwood from hardwood is by the closeness of the grain. The grain is identified by the lines running along the timber. In hardwood, the lines are very close together. When timber is cut into boards, it is cut with the grain running along the length of the board.

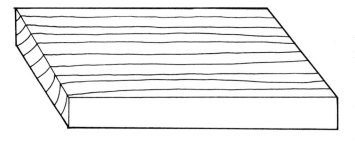

BUYING WOOD

If you are buying your wood from a timber merchant or DIY shop, one word of warning . . . When a piece of wood is sold, as, for example 1in x 1in (25mm x 25mm)* that is the size of the wood when it is still rough-sawn. If the wood is then planed on all four surfaces, it will be reduced in each dimension, usually by ⅛in (3mm), but in some instances, by as much as ¼in (6mm). Take care, therefore, when you order wood, that after it has been cut and planed, it is the exact length and size you require. This applies to all sizes of planed wood.

Other points to be considered when you select your wood:

1. It should not have too many knots in it. It is almost impossible to get wood without at least one knot in it, but the fewer the better, because a knot in the wrong place (for example, in a handle or leg) can weaken the wood and cause it to break if too much pressure is applied.

2. It should not be badly warped or twisted, as this can cause problems when you try to align two pieces together: for example on an easel, or when jointing two pieces of wood together, where one piece rocks because of the warp.

3. It should have no damaged edges, either because it has been knocked or banged, or because in the process of planing the wood from the rough side, the machine has missed some areas.

The metric measurement is given throughout this book to the nearest millimetre. For example, 1 inch equals 25.4mm, but this is given as 25mm.

SHEET MATERIALS

Plywood, chipboard and hardboard are sold in sheets, e.g., 8ft x 4ft (240cm x 120cm) or 6ft x 3ft (180cm x 90cm).

Plywood is made up of several thin layers of wood glued together. Each layer has the grain running in alternate directions to the layer next to it, but the outside layers run in the same direction. Consequently, plywood is made up of odd numbers of layers. Plywood is available in thicknesses of up to 1in (25mm).

Chipboard is made by bonding resin-coated wood particles together under high pressure. Chipboard is available in thicknesses usually from ½in to 1in (12mm to 25mm).

Hardboard is made from softwood pulp which is made into sheets by bonding under high pressure. The most common thicknesses of hardboard are ⅛in, 3/16in, and ¼in (3mm, 4mm and 6mm).

CUTTING WOOD

When cutting wood or sheet materials it is important to choose the correct saw.

Wood. If you cut across the grain, use a crosscut or panel saw for rough cuts, or a tenon saw. The tenon saw will leave a smooth surface across the end of the timber. If you cut along the grain of the wood, a ripsaw can be used. This is more efficient for this job as it has larger teeth than the other saws.

Plywood. For cutting plywood up to a thickness of ½in (12mm) use a tenon saw. Above ½in (12mm) a panel saw can be used. Always cut on the face side of the plywood when you are cutting across the grain of the top layer, as there will inevitably be some splintering of the underside.

Chipboard. To cut chipboard, a panel or tenon saw can be used, and as with plywood, the face side should be cut.

Hardboard. To cut hardboard, always use a tenon saw, and again, only cut on the face side. To prevent the hardboard sheet from tearing when being sawn, it must be well supported on the underside. Do not saw too quickly, or force the saw, as this will tend to tear the sheet. Take care not to score the surface of the hardboard as it is impossible to remove the marks later.

When you cut any type of wood or sheet material, the saw should be held vertical to the piece of wood or sheet material being cut. With wood and the thicker type of sheet material, a vertical line should be marked on the edge and a line squared across the face of the piece of wood to ensure that the cut is square and vertical.

TYPES OF JOINT

The essence of all jointing is accurate marking out. Always check the marking out twice, as wood, once cut wrongly, is wasted. Many types of joint can be used to fix two pieces of wood together. The ones I used to construct the toys in this book are described as follows:-

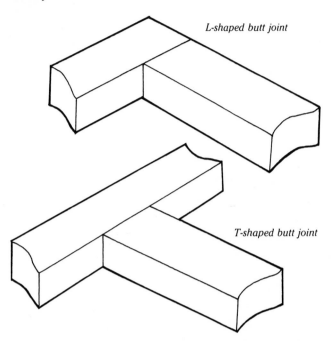

L-shaped butt joint

T-shaped butt joint

L and T-shaped butt joints. The commonest type of joint is the simple butt joint. This consists of two pieces of wood, the cross piece with the end cut dead square, butted up to the second piece of timber. If the two pieces of wood are joined at the ends, this forms an L shape; if the cross piece is in the middle, this forms a T shape. The joints should be glued, and, if necessary, screwed together.

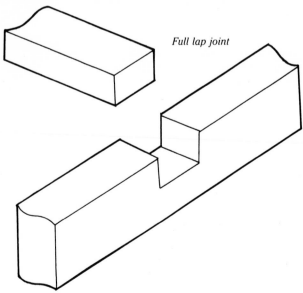

Full lap joint

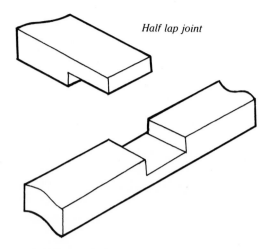

Half lap joint

Full and half lap joints. These joints are stronger and neater than the simple butt joints. The full lap joint is where the exact shape of the cross piece is cut out of the side piece. When fitted together, the top of the cross piece is level with the top of the side piece.

The joint can be completed by simply glueing, or, if extra strength is required, by glueing and screwing.

The half lap joint is, as the name indicates, where half of each piece of wood is removed so that when the joint is assembled, the pieces of wood are flush with each other. This type of joint can be used to form an L-shape or a T-shape. As with the full lap, it can be both glued and screwed.

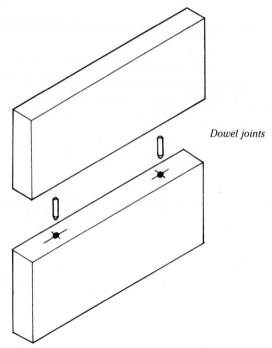

Dowel joints

Dowel joints. These can be used to join wood together, edge to edge, to produce a wider piece of wood. They are strong joints and are relatively easy to make. They are made by drilling holes on the edges of two pieces of wood, inserting small dowels in the holes of one piece of wood, and locating the dowels in the corresponding holes in the second piece of wood. With this type of joint, it is important that the holes are in line with each other; otherwise the surfaces of the wood at the join will not be flush with each other.

To mark the centres of the dowel holes, clamp both boards together back to back, and using a marking gauge and the metal square (see Tools, page 8) mark a centre line the length of the wood used and square lines across the wood at 6in (150mm) intervals.

The holes should be drilled vertically and slightly deeper than the length of the dowel to be used. Chamfer the ends of each dowel and also cut a groove in the length of the dowel. This should allow any excess glue to escape from the hole when the wood is clamped together. If this is not done and there is too much glue in the hole when the dowels are inserted, the pressure might split the surface of the wood.

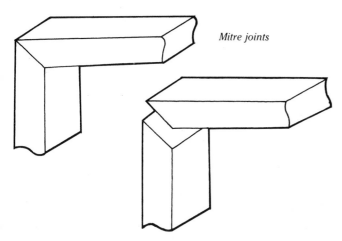

Mitre joints

Mitre joints. Mitre joints are made by cutting 45-degree angles at the end of each piece of wood. These have to be cut accurately so as to form a 90-degree angle when joined together. This type of joint is used for forming squares. It gives a neat appearance to external corners.

To cut a mitre joint, it is advisable to use a multi-purpose jointing jig (see Tools, page 9). With this, the saw and the piece of wood are held securely in place by guides. The saw is worked through the guides to give an accurate vertical cut.

Mortice and tenon joints. A mortice and tenon joint is a strong joint, but it is not easy to construct. The joint has a mortice hole cut in one piece of wood and the tenon cut on the other piece of wood. The tenon fits into the mortice hole. To make this joint you need a mortice marking gauge (see Tools). Set the two points on the mortice marking gauge to the thickness of the tenon. This should not be less than one-third of the thickness of the wood being used. Mark the width of the tenon on the piece of wood where the mortice hole is to be cut. Square these lines all around the wood. With the marking gauge, mark the tenon on one piece of wood and the mortice hole on the other up to the lines squared around the wood.

Cut the tenon with a tenon saw. Make the tenon long enough to project just beyond the mortice hole to allow for smoothing off after assembly. Make the mortice hole by drilling out the wood between the parallel lines with either a twist drill or brace and bit (see Tools section), and remove the remainder of the wood from the mortice hole with a chisel.

When assembled and clamped together, wedges can be inserted to add strength to the joint. If this is done, the mortice hole should be enlarged by ⅛in (3mm) on each

side to accommodate the wedges. This enlargement should not go the complete depth of the mortice hole, but should be tapered off to nothing three-quarters of the way through (see diagrams 1-5 below).

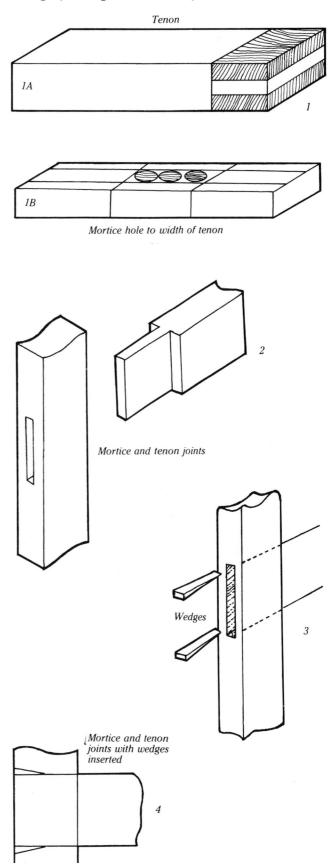

Tenon

1A *1*

1B

Mortice hole to width of tenon

2

Mortice and tenon joints

Wedges

3

Mortice and tenon joints with wedges inserted

4

15

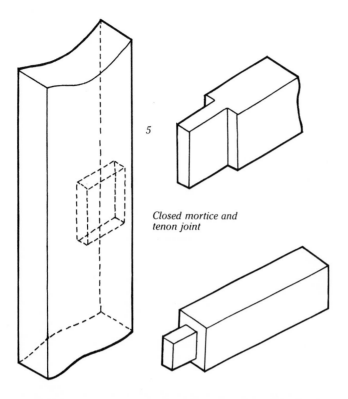

Closed mortice and
tenon joint

There are many variations of the mortice and tenon
joint, but one of the most useful is the closed mortice and
tenon joint. In this, the mortice hole does not go all the
way through the wood and the tenon is cut to slightly less
than the depth of the mortice hole. This type of mortice
and tenon gives a neater look to the joint if the outside
edge of the work is visible.

Another variation of the mortice and tenon joint is
when the tenon has a shoulder cut on all four sides. This
reduces the strength of the tenon a little, but again, it
gives it a much neater appearance.

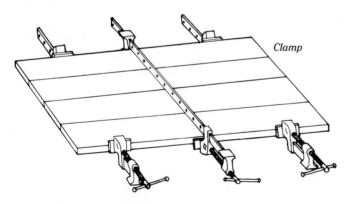

Clamp

CLAMPING/CRAMPING

When joints are glued, they usually need to be clamped
together to allow the glue to set. With all types of clamping, a lot of pressure is applied to the surface of the wood.
To avoid damage to the piece of work, therefore, insert
some pieces of waste wood where the pressure is to be applied. For types of clamp, see Tools, pages 9-10.

For clamping work, usually two clamps are needed. Apply even pressure to each clamp alternately until the
two surfaces are in contact with each other, and you can

see the glue oozing from the joints. Do not over-tighten
the clamp as this can distort the clamp and/or wood.

After clamping make sure that the surface of the work
or the framework is level and not distorted.

GLUES

There are many excellent wood glues available. Try out a
number of these to decide which you find best to work
with. Usually, these glues can be wiped off the surface of
the wood with a damp cloth within ten minutes of use, and
will not stain the wood. To achieve the best result, follow
the manufacturer's instructions carefully. If the toy you
are glueing is likely to be used out-of-doors and exposed
to the elements, ensure that the glue you use is suitable to
resist this.

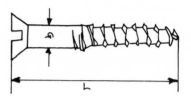

SCREWS

The only type of screw I have used is one with a counter-
sunk flat head. Screws are made from various types of
metal, for example mild steel and brass, and they are
available in numerous sizes and thicknesses (or gauge,
which is measured as the diameter of its shank.) Its length
is from the tip of the thread to the top of the head.

Always choose the correct gauge and length of a screw
when screwing two pieces of wood together as a screw
that is too thick will split the wood and a screw that is too
long will go through both pieces of wood and the tip will
be visible and could be dangerous.

When screwing two pieces of wood together, drill a
pilot hole, the thickness of the gauge of the screw, into
one piece of wood and with this held in position, push a
bradawl through the pilot hole and puncture the surface
of the second piece of wood. This will allow the screw to
enter the second piece of wood easily.

Also at this stage, using a countersink bit, countersink
the pilot hole so that when the screw is fitted, the head is
flush with or just below the surface of the wood. This will
eliminate any possibility of scratching or catching oneself.

When you screw two pieces of wood together of different thicknesses, always drill the pilot hole in the thin-
ner piece of wood and screw into the thicker one.

FILLING

When the toys have been assembled any screw holes or
small gaps should be filled with a good quality filler. For
toys that are intended for outside use an external cellulose
filler should be used.

When filling, always leave the filler slightly raised
above the surface of the wood to allow for sanding down.

SANDING

This term is misleading in that abrasive papers are no
longer coated with sand but with crushed glass.

Sandpaper, or glasspaper is available in various grades from coarse to fine. The way to obtain the smooth finish required is to start with a coarse paper and work down through to the finer grades.

It is advisable to use sandpaper with a cork block to obtain a smooth flat finish. Wrap the sandpaper around the block and rub the block and paper together up and down along the grain of the wood. Do not rub across the grain as this will leave scratch marks which will be visible if the wood is varnished.

A power sanding machine will help a great deal if you have a large area to smooth down. In awkward corners, where the block or a power sander cannot reach, you will have to apply finger pressure to the sandpaper to obtain the finish required.

PAINTING

All primers, undercoats and gloss paints must be lead-free and non-toxic. All tins of paint carry extensive instructions regarding application as well as health and safety precautions. These should be read carefully and followed when applying the paint.

When toys are intended for outside use, firstly prime the wood with a good quality wood primer. When this is dry, rub down lightly with a fine grade glasspaper. This will give a good 'key' to the next coat of paint. Apply the undercoat and, when dry, repeat the sanding operation. This ensures a good base for the gloss coats and provides a smooth finish. The gloss coats, preferably two, should be of an exterior quality paint.

For interior use, toys should be treated in the same way, but one coat of gloss paint will suffice.

VARNISH

When varnishing, check that the varnish will adhere to the wood you are using. This can be done by applying the varnish you intend to use to a piece of scrap wood from the toy.

Never use old varnish. This can dry with a 'milky' look, ruining the appearance of the toy and necessitating the stripping and revarnishing of the entire surface.

I have used exterior gloss varnish on all the toys that had natural wood finishes. To give a strong smooth finish, I applied three coats, sanding lightly between each coat.

With toys that have wheels, I found it easier to paint some of the parts before assembly. Before you complete the assembly of any toy, check and find any parts you think will be easier to paint or varnish beforehand.

1
SIMPLE TOYS

Boat. A good model to start on.

BOAT

Boats are always popular with children, whether they are sailing little boats in the bath, on a pond, or in the sea. This simple model can be made easily, and will give hours of enjoyment.

DIAGRAM 1 (see opposite)

Base. On the surface of the main base of the boat (1), on the 4in (100mm) surface, draw a centre line lengthwise. At the rear (stern) of the boat, mark out a semi-circle. At the front of the boat (bows) make a mark 2½in (62mm) from the end on each side. Connect these two points to the centre line, mark on the end, to form a 'v' shape.

On the centre line 1½in (37mm) from the front and 1in (25mm) from the back, mark the funnel centres.

The shape can now be cut out using a coping saw. It is advisable to round the bows of the boat so as not to leave too sharp a point.

DIAGRAM 2

Drill the two ½in (12mm) holes for the funnels. To do this, place the drill on the mark and drill into the timber ⅛in (3mm). Then tilt the drill to the required angle of the fun-

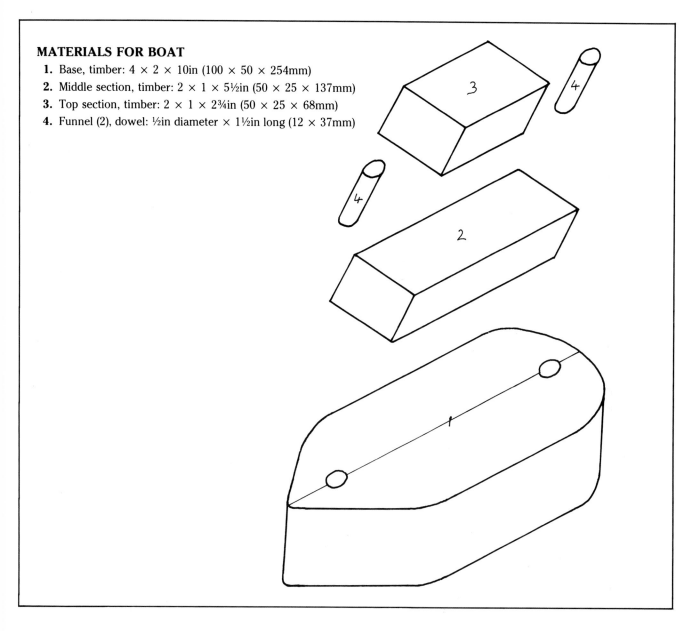

MATERIALS FOR BOAT

1. Base, timber: 4 × 2 × 10in (100 × 50 × 254mm)
2. Middle section, timber: 2 × 1 × 5½in (50 × 25 × 137mm)
3. Top section, timber: 2 × 1 × 2¾in (50 × 25 × 68mm)
4. Funnel (2), dowel: ½in diameter × 1½in long (12 × 37mm)

nel and continue to drill at this angle to a depth of ½in (12mm).

DIAGRAM 3

Top and middle sections. Make the top sections from the pieces of timber (2 and 3). On both pieces, cut the ends to the same angle as the boat's funnels. In all cases, I used a 60-degree angle. Glue the two pieces together and then fix them on to the base in the centre of the timber and between the funnels. Cut two pieces of ½in (12mm) dowel (4) 1½in (37mm) along, and fit these into the holes in the base to represent the funnels.

The whole assembly should now be well sanded down with sandpaper to remove any sharp edges and the tops of the funnels chamfered off. The boat can then be painted using a good quality exterior paint to withstand immersion in water.

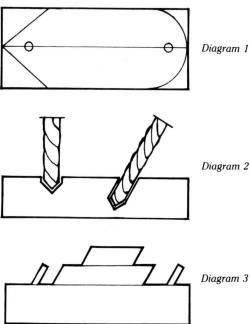

Diagram 1

Diagram 2

Diagram 3

BUILDING BLOCKS IN BOX

This toy is easily made with the basic tools and, depending on how confident you feel, the size, shape and quantity of the building blocks can be varied to any combination.

A mosaic of building bricks in their box.

DIAGRAM 1 (page 22)

The box. Make the box from the chipboard base (1) and the four pieces of timber (2). Each piece of timber for the sides (2) has a mitre cut on each end, as this gives a better looking finish to the box.

After the mitres have been cut on each of the sides, assemble the sides on the base. The sides should be flush with the outside edges of the base, and be perfectly square. This can be done by checking the two diagonal measurements. When this is achieved, glue and screw each side into position.

MATERIALS FOR BUILDING BLOCKS IN BOX

Box

1. Base, chipboard: 13¾ × 13¾ × ½in (350 × 350 × 12mm)
2. Sides, timber: 13¾ × ⅞ × ⅞in (350 × 22 × 22mm)

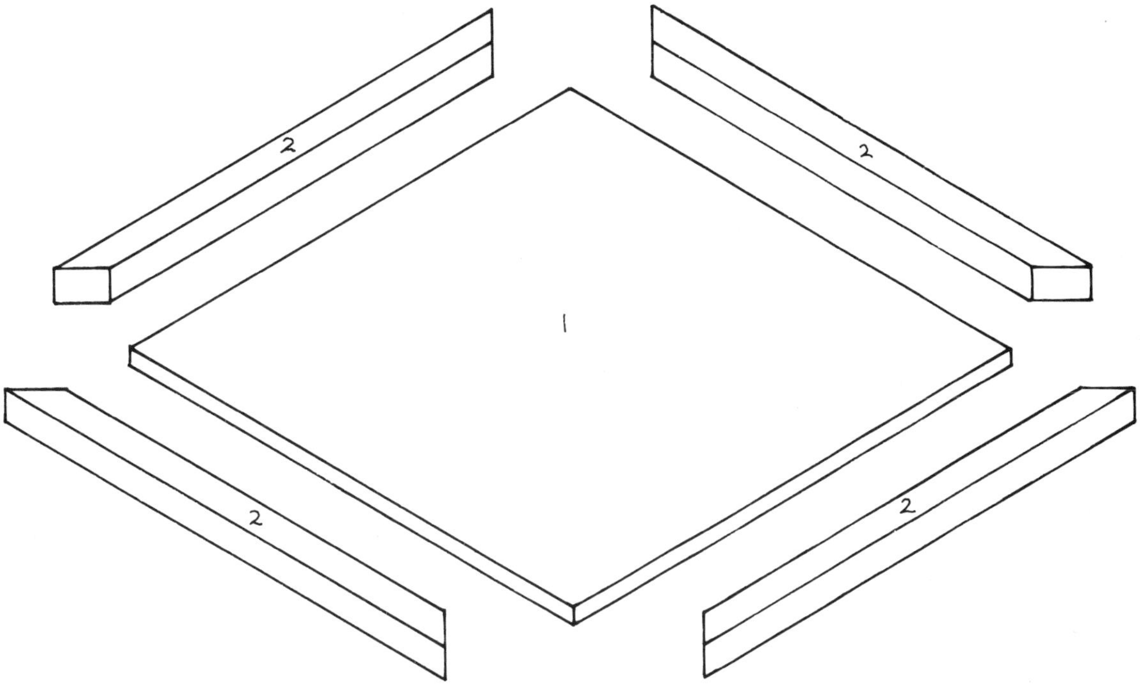

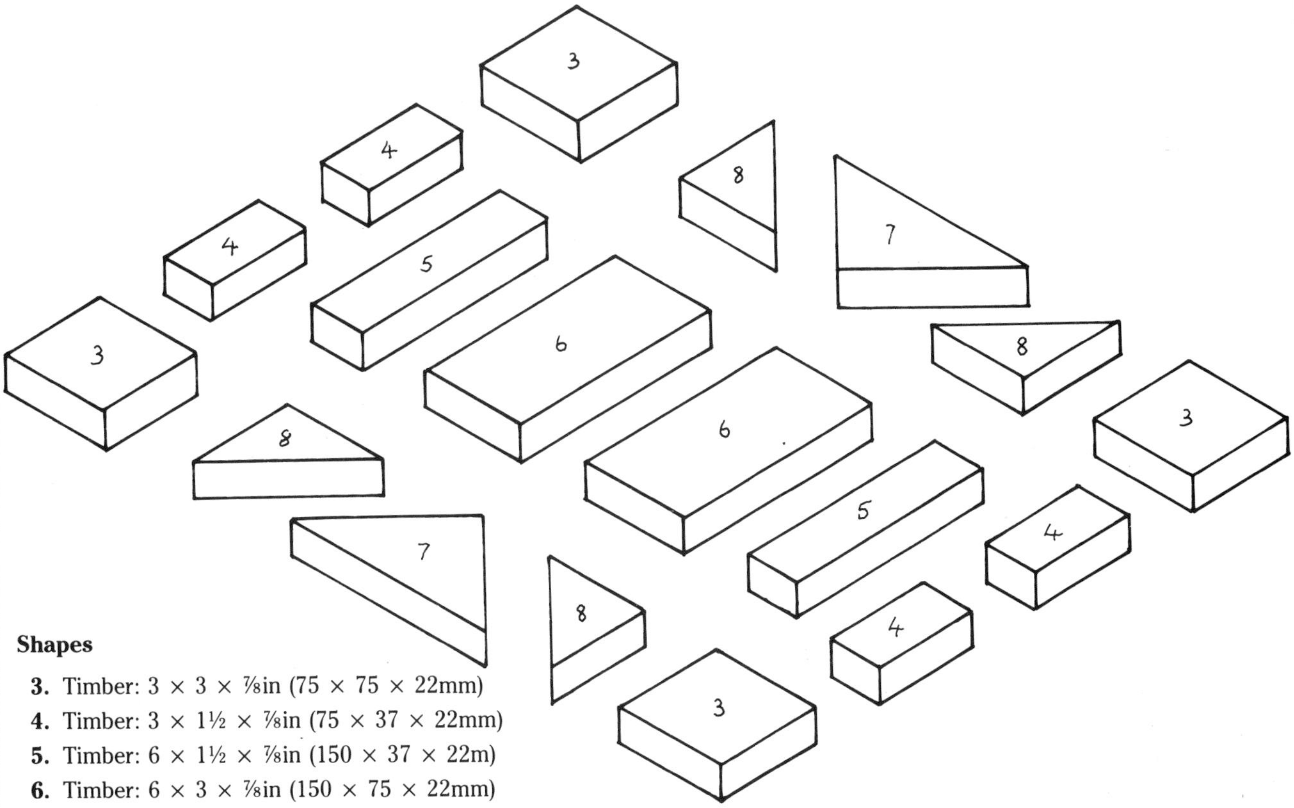

Shapes

3. Timber: 3 × 3 × ⅞in (75 × 75 × 22mm)
4. Timber: 3 × 1½ × ⅞in (75 × 37 × 22mm)
5. Timber: 6 × 1½ × ⅞in (150 × 37 × 22m)
6. Timber: 6 × 3 × ⅞in (150 × 75 × 22mm)
7. Timber triangle: 6 × 3 × ⅞in (150 × 75 × 22mm)
8. Timber triangle: 3 × 3 × ⅞in (75 × 75 × 22mm)
   Large-headed ½in (12mm) brass pins (2)

DIAGRAM 2

The building blocks. The shape of the blocks:-
First mark these out on a piece of paper measuring the same as the inside of the box. In this way, the number and shape of the blocks can be arranged to be as simple or as complicated as you wish. Cut the paper into the shapes drawn and place one shape on a piece of ⅞in (22mm) thick timber (3 and 8) and mark out the shape. Then cut out the shape with a tenon saw, doing so just inside the line marked to allow for the painting of the shape.

DIAGRAM 3

Of the shapes to be used, choose a shape or a matching pair of shapes and hammer a large headed brass pin into the centre of the shape. This allows the shape to be pulled easily out of the box.

Using a fine grade sandpaper, sand down the box and individual blocks and paint to the colours of your choice.

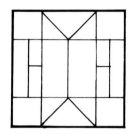

Diagram 2

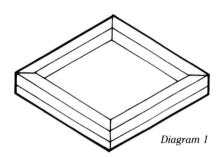

Diagram 1

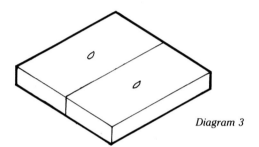

Diagram 3

22

DOLL'S BED AND CRADLE

Along with her dolls, a cradle is probably a small girl's most treasured possession. This particular design has a detachable base, which gives the toy a dual purpose, i.e. as a bed and a cradle.

Doll's cradle. Goodnight, sweet princess.

DIAGRAM 1 (page 24)

Bed. Mark and cut out the two endpieces (1), as shown.

DIAGRAM 2

Cut the sides (2) to length with a tenon saw and, with a smoothing plane, round off the top inside edges. Glue and screw the two ends and the sides together. The top of the two sides should finish level with the shoulders of the ends. This will leave a portion of the sides' bottom edges protruding below the endpieces. Remove this with a smoothing plane.

DIAGRAM 3

Cut the base (3) to length and mark the angle on each edge. With a smoothing plane, shape the base to fit into place between the two sides. Glue the base in position.

DIAGRAM 4

Cradle. Mark and cut the two endpieces (4). To do this, clamp both pieces of timber together and cut to shape with a coping saw. This will ensure that both ends are the same shape. 1in (25mm) down from the top of the endpieces, in the centre, mark the shape of the bed and cut out this section with a coping saw.

DIAGRAM 5

Cut the central support piece (5) to length. Glue and screw two endpieces to the central support. Ensure that the top of the support piece is flush with the bottom of the recess in the endpieces and that the overall length is the same as the cot.

Sand down and paint each section separately. For added decoration, you can either paint or stencil colourful patterns or bunches of flowers on each end and the sides.

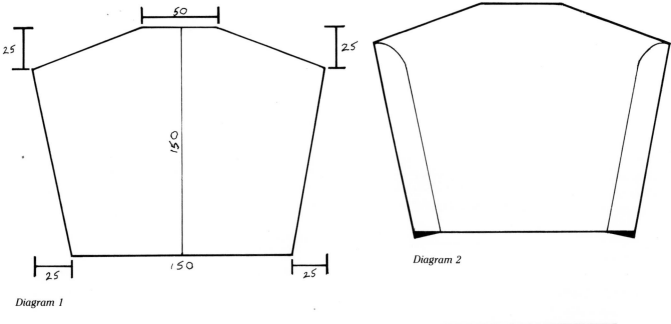

Diagram 1

Diagram 2

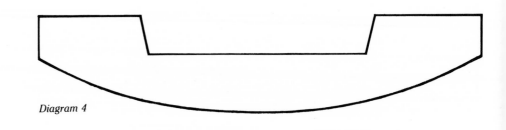

Diagram 3

Diagram 4

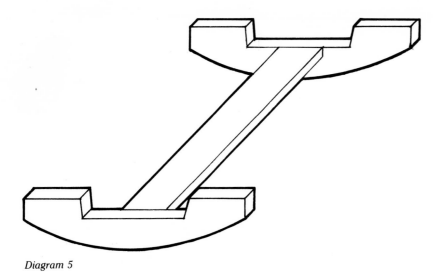

Diagram 5

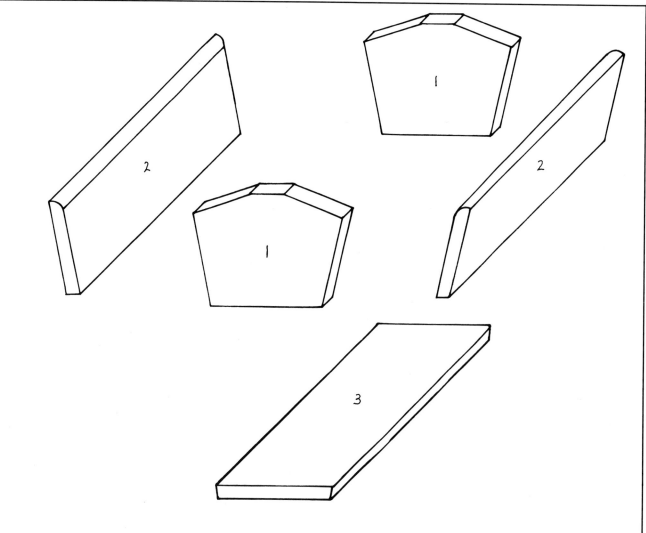

MATERIALS FOR BED AND CRADLE

Bed

1. Ends (2), timber: 8 × 6 × ⅝in (203 × 150 × 15mm)
2. Sides (2), timber: 12 × 5 × ⅝in (305 × 125 × 15mm)
3. Base (1), timber: 12 × 5 × ⅝in (305 × 125 × 15mm)

Cradle

4. End pieces (2), timber: 12 × 2½ × ⅝in (305 × 62 × 15mm)
5. Central support: 12 × 2½ × ⅝in (305 × 62 × 15mm) timber

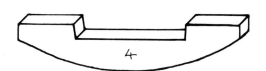

ROCKET

Since the advent of space travel, let alone science fiction, a rocket has been almost a compulsory addition to a child's playbox.

DIAGRAM 1 (see below)

Base. Cut the base (1) to size with a tenon saw and mark the centre by drawing diagonal lines. In the centre, drill out a ½in (12mm) hole with a twist bit, ensuring that the hole is vertical. Cut the centre support dowel (2) to length, and glue this in position in the hole in the base. Ensure the dowel is flush with the bottom of the base. The top of the dowel should be rounded.

DIAGRAM 2

Fuselage sections. Cut the six fuselage sections (3 and 4) to size. In the centre of each, drill a ⅝in (15mm) hole with a twist bit. Ensure that the holes are drilled vertically. When this is done, check that each section will move up and down the central dowel easily. When all sections are in position on the dowel, ensure that there is ½in (12mm) still protruding. On the three square sections of the fuselage, on two outside faces, cut ¼in (6mm) grooves to a depth of ¼in (6mm). Cut the fins (5) to shape with a tenon saw and glue these in position in the grooves.

DIAGRAM 3

Nose cone. Cut the nose cone (6) to shape using a coping saw and, in the centre of the base, drill a ½in (12mm) hole. This should fit tightly on top of the central support dowel.

Sand down and paint each section. To give added pleasure, each section can be painted a different colour.

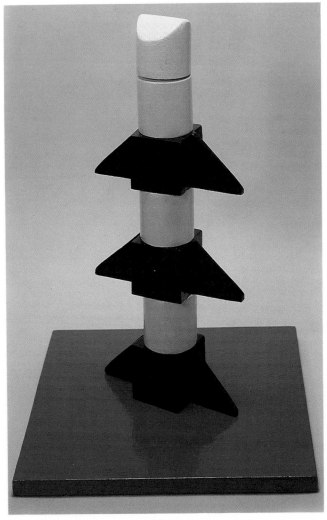

Five, four, three, two, one. Action!

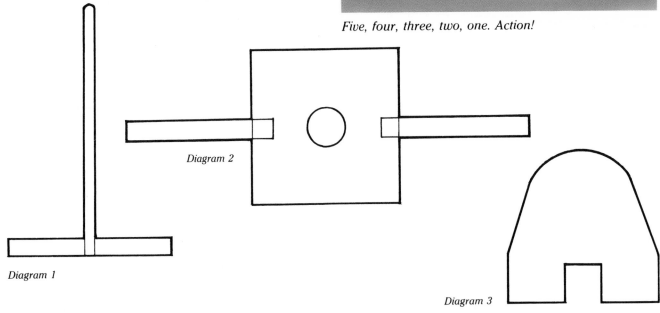

Diagram 1

Diagram 2

Diagram 3

MATERIALS FOR ROCKET

1. Base, plywood: 9 × 9 × ⅞in (229 × 229 × 22mm)
2. Centre support, dowel: 13 × ½in diameter (330 × 12mm)

Fuselage sections

3. (3), timber: 2 × 2 × 2in (50 × 50 × 50mm)
4. (3), dowel: 2in diameter (50mm)
5. Fins, plywood: 2 × 2 × ¼in (50 × 50 × 6mm)
6. Nose cone, timber: 2 × 2 × 2in (50 × 50 × 50mm)

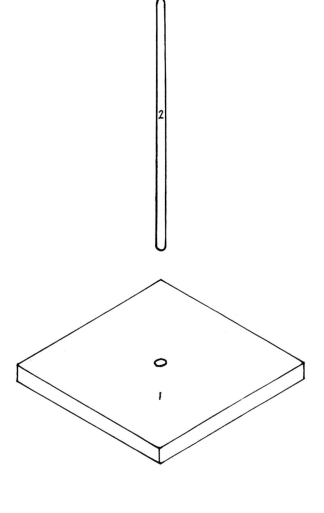

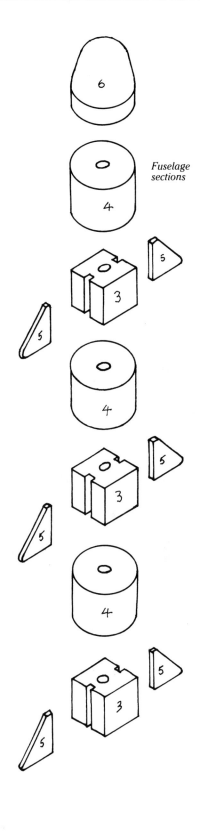

Fuselage sections

VEGETABLE PUZZLE

This puzzle, a variation of the normal jigsaw, is a novel item. I have used three vegetable shapes but, depending on your skill with a coping saw, any number of different vegetable or fruit shapes may be cut.

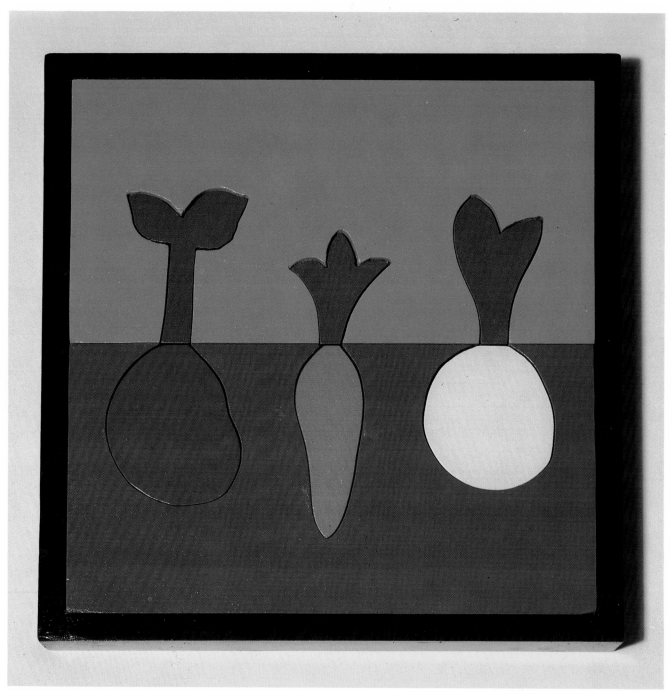

A novel jigsaw for the very young

Box. Construct base (1) and sides (2) of the box in exactly the same way as for the Building Blocks in Box (page 20). Ensure that the box is perfectly square.

DIAGRAM (see page 30)

Puzzle inserts. Mark and cut out the two main inserts (1). Ensure that these two inserts fit easily into the box. Remove the two inserts, and on one half, mark out the vegetable shapes desired. Cut these shapes out with a cop-

MATERIALS FOR VEGETABLE PUZZLE
Box (as for Building blocks, page 20)

Base, chipboard: 13¾ × 13¾ × ½in (350 × 350 × 12mm)
Sides (4), timber: 13¾ × ⅞ × ⅞in (350 × 22 × 22mm)

Puzzle Inserts

1. (2), timber: 12 × 6 × ⅞in (305 × 150 × 22mm)
   Round-headed ½in (12mm) brass nails (2)

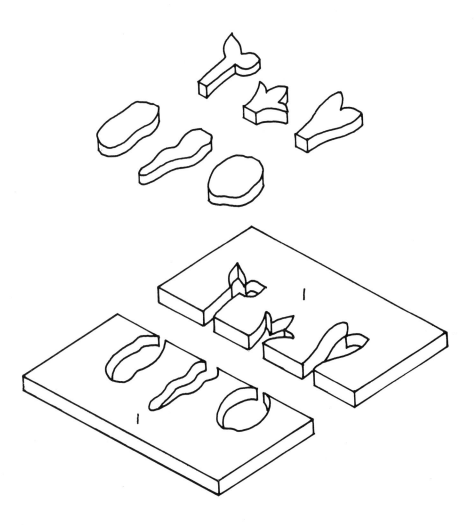

ing saw. As the toy is for smaller children, avoid cutting too intricate a shape. On the second insert, directly opposite each vegetable, mark and cut out the foliage.

Sand down the shapes and the internal facing of the cut-out on the main sections. To represent the earth, paint the bottom inserts brown, with the vegetable shapes cut out, and paint·the vegetables the appropriate colours. To represent the sky, paint the main insert (with the foliage cut out) light blue and the foliage green. If you apply more than one coat of paint, check that each shape will fit into its corresponding hole without sticking. If difficulty is experienced in removing each shape, then ease the hole in the main inserts with sandpaper.

To assist in removing the shapes, fix round-headed brass nails into the centre of each, as with the Building Blocks (page 20).

Diagram

2
TOYS WITH WHEELS

RAILWAY ENGINE

Railway engines are, if anything, even more popular with children (and adults) since the departure of steam. This model of a small tank engine can be made easily and cheaply, and when painted in attractive colours, will become a perennial favourite.

DIAGRAM 1

Locomotive body. Make the body of the locomotive from the timber base (1), the side pieces (2), the top (3) and front (4). Glue the pieces to the base, ensuring that the sides are vertical. Glue the top and front to the sides.

DIAGRAM 2

Locomotive cab. The cab consists of the front (5) two sides (6), the rear piece (7) and the roof (8). In the front of the cab, mark and drill two ½in (12mm) holes at a position of ¾in (18mm) from the top, and ½in (12mm) from each edge. Drill these holes to a depth of ½in (12mm).

DIAGRAM 3

On the cab sides 1in (25mm) from the top and 2in (50mm) from the bottom, mark and cut out a 1¾in (32mm) deep piece to represent the side lookouts. To ensure that these lookouts are identical, clamp the two pieces of wood together in the bench vice and cut them both out together. Use a coping saw to round the inside corners.

DIAGRAM 4 (see page 32)

The tank front and sides can now be glued to the main base of the locomotive. Glue the rear piece and the roof to the cab rear and top.

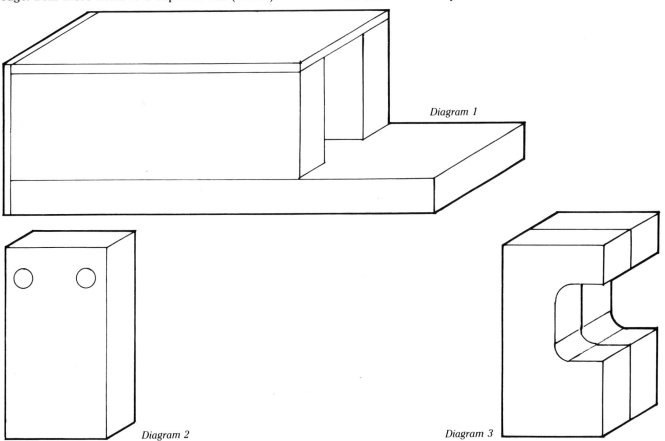

Diagram 1

Diagram 2

Diagram 3

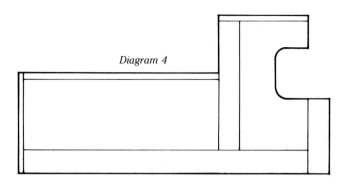

Diagram 4

DIAGRAM 7

3in (75mm) in from the end of the chassis piece on the bottom, drill two ⅜in (10mm) holes to a depth of ½in (12mm). Replace the ⅜in (10mm) drill with a ¼in (6mm) drill, and in the same holes, drill completely through the chassis. The chassis pieces can now be screwed to the underside of the base of the locomotive, using 1½in (37mm) gauge 8 screws. The chassis should be ¼in (6mm) in from each end of the locomotive body.

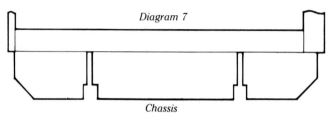

Diagram 7

Chassis

DIAGRAM 5

Locomotive chassis. On the chassis piece of timber (9), 1in (25mm) from the top at each end, mark a 45-degree angle and, with a tenon saw, cut off these corner pieces. Mark the centres of the holes for the axles ⅜in (10mm) from the bottom of the chassis piece, one in the centre and the other two 4in (100mm) either side. On these marks, drill ⅜in (10mm) holes vertically through the chassis piece.

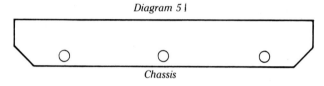

Diagram 5

Chassis

DIAGRAM 6

Cut the three axles (10) to length and, with the hole saw, cut six 2in (50mm) diameter wheels (11). Glue the axles into the wheels on one side, ensuring that the axle is flush with the outside of the wheel.

Place each axle through the hole in the chassis and fit the other wheels on to the axles, again ensuring that the axle is flush with the outside of the wheel. The wheels should not be glued in position permanently at this stage, as it is easier to paint the whole locomotive first. Check that the chassis assembly runs smoothly.

DIAGRAM 8

Take the two buffer beams (12) and, on the two bottom corners, mark a ½in (12mm) radius circle and cut the corners of the buffer beam to shape with a coping saw. Glue the buffer beams to the ends of the chassis pieces, ensuring that they are flush with the sides of the locomotive. Glue the buffers (13) in the centre of the buffer beam, ⅝in (15mm) in from each edge.

Glue the circular piece of timber (14) in the centre on the front of the locomotive to represent the smoke box door. Glue the two pieces of dowel (15 and 16) on the top of the locomotive body to represent a chimney and a safety valve.

The whole assembly should now be sanded with fine graded sandpaper and painted. Take special care not to allow paint to run into the axle holes.

Finally, the axles can be inserted in each hole and the second wheels glued in position with the axle flush with the outside edge. It may be necessary to add a dab of paint on to the end of the axle to complete the painting.

Diagram 8

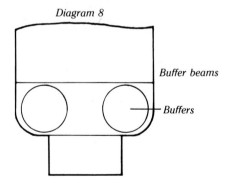

Buffer beams

Buffers

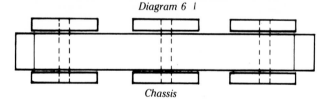

Diagram 6

Chassis

MATERIALS FOR RAILWAY ENGINE

Locomotive Body

1. Base, timber: ⅞ × 11¼ × 2¾in (22 × 287 × 70mm)
2. Side pieces (2), timber: ⅞ × 8 × 2¾in (22 × 203 × 70mm)
3. Top, plywood: 8 × 2¾ × ¼in (203 × 70 × 6mm)
4. Front, plywood: 2¾ × 3⅞ × ¼in (70 × 98 × 6mm)

Locomotive cab

5. Front, timber: ⅞ × 2¾ × 5in (22 × 70 × 125mm)
6. Sides (2), timber: ⅞ × 2¾ × 5in (22 × 70 × 125mm)
7. Rear, timber: ⅞ × 2⅞ × 2¾in (22 × 72 × 70mm)
8. Roof, plywood: 2¾ × 3½ × ¼in (70 × 90 × 6mm)

Locomotive Chassis

9. Chassis, timber: 12 × 1¼ × 1¾in (305 × 33 × 45mm)
10. Axles (3), dowel: 2⅝ × ⅜in diameter (68 × 10mm)
11. Wheels (6), timber: ⅝ × 2⅜in diameter (15 × 60mm)
12. Buffer beams (2), plywood: 2¾ × 1 × ¼in (70 × 25 × 6mm)
13. Buffers (4), dowel: ½ × ⅞in diameter (12 × 22mm)
14. Smoke box, dowel: ¼ × 1¾in diameter (6 × 45mm)
15. Chimney, dowel: 1 × ⅞in diameter (25 × 22mm)
16. Safety valve, dowel: 1 × ⅞in diameter (25 × 22mm)

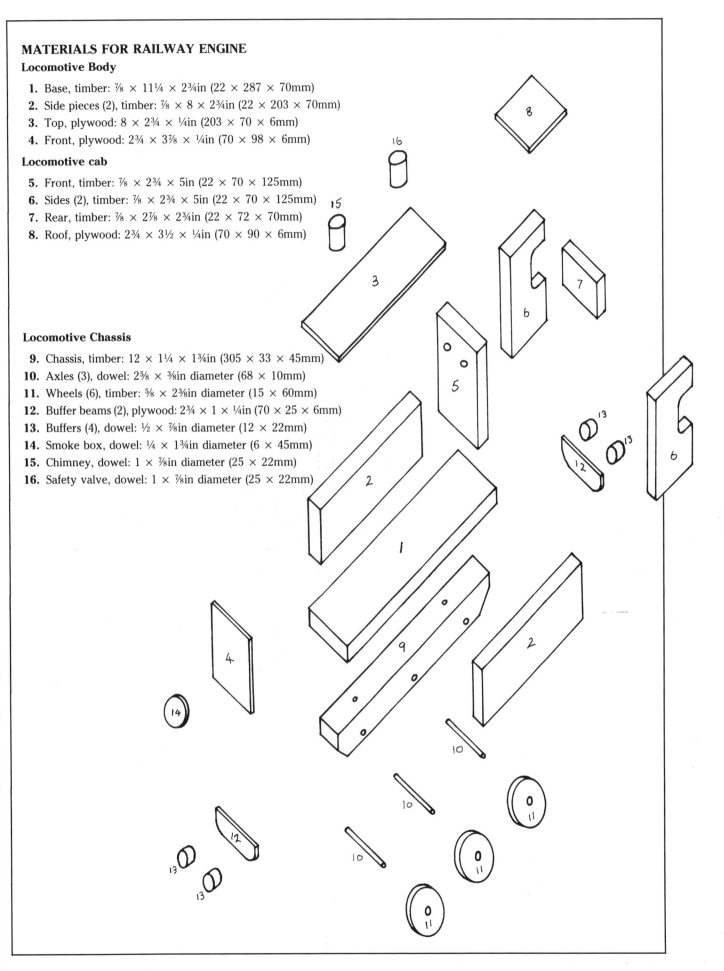

33

TANK

All aspiring soldiers, girls and boys, will want to possess and drive their own tank just as much as their own car. Making this one is not as complicated as one might think.

DIAGRAM 1

Main body. Make the main body of the tank from the five pieces of timber (1). On one of these pieces, mark out the shape of the tank. Clamp all five pieces together with two G clamps (US. 'C' clamps) and cut out the shape.

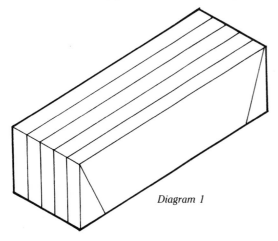

Diagram 1

DIAGRAM 2

Remove the two outside pieces and glue the middle three pieces together. Mark and cut out the recesses for the three wheels (2).

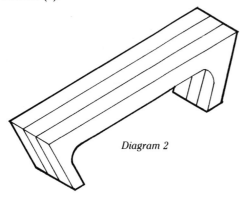

Diagram 2

DIAGRAM 3

On the two outside pieces mark out the holes for the wheels. Drill the holes 1in (25mm) in diameter and to a depth of ½in (12mm) with a twist bit.

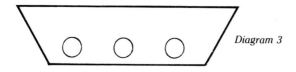

Diagram 3

A tank, a tank engine, and a lorry that seems to have shed a brick or two.

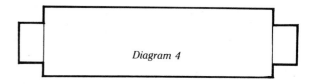

Diagram 4

DIAGRAM 4

Glue one of the outside pieces to the three centre pieces in line with the shape. Take the three pieces of dowel for the wheels (2) and with the hole saw reduce the ends of each dowel to 1in (25mm) and to a depth of ⅝in (15mm). Cut away the outside waste with a tenon saw.

Insert the wheels into the holes in the side-piece, and place the second side-piece in position, locating the wheels in the holes in this piece. Simply by holding the second side-piece in position, check that the wheels revolve freely. If they do not, then remove the wheels and sand down each end until they do. When the wheels revolve freely, glue the second side-piece in position. When the glue has dried, mark and drill a ⅜in (10mm) hole in the centre of the top to a depth of ½in (12mm).

DIAGRAM 5 (see next page)

Turret. Cut the piece of timber for the turret (3) and chamfer all edges to leave a ⅜in (10mm) surface. On the top of the turret in the centre, drill a ⅜in (10mm) hole right through the timber. Ensure the hole is drilled vertically.

On the front of the turret in the centre and ⅝in (15mm) from the top, drill another ½in (12mm) hole to a depth of ½in (12mm) to house the barrel (4). Cut the piece of dowel for the barrel to length and glue this into the position in the hole.

DIAGRAM 6

With the hole saw, cut out the disc (5). This will have a ⅜in (10mm) hole in the centre. Cut the pivot dowel (6) to length and glue it into the hole in the disc. Ensure that the

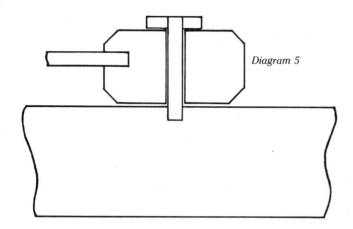

Diagram 5

end of the dowel is flush with the top of the disc.

Put a dab of glue in the bottom of the hole in the main body and place the turret in position over it. Insert the pivot dowel and disc through the turret and into the hole in the main body. Ensure the turret revolves freely.

Cut the eight plywood discs (7), and glue them in position on the body sides. Sand down and paint to colours of your choice.

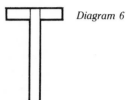

Diagram 6

MATERIALS FOR TANK

1. Main Body, timber: 12 × 3 × ⅞in (300 × 75 × 22mm)
2. Wheels (3), dowel: 3⅞ × 1¾in diameter (97 × 45mm)
3. Turret (1), timber: 4 × 3 × 2in (100 × 75 × 50mm)
4. Barrel (1), dowel: 5½ × ½in diameter (140 × 12mm)
5. Turret disc (1), timber: 1½ diameter × ⅜in (37 × 10mm)
6. Pivot dowel, dowel: 2½ × ⅜in diameter (62 × 10mm)
7. Side discs, plywood: 1¾ diameter × 3/16in (45 × 4mm)

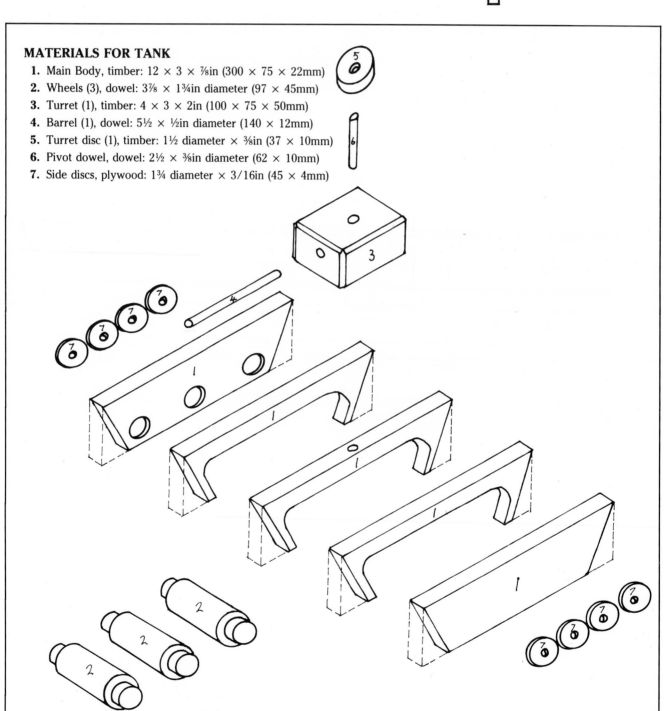

TRUCK WITH BRICKS

All children like to have a solidly built truck or lorry to push about. This one incorporates its load as well, multi-coloured bricks as in 'Building blocks in box'.

DIAGRAM 1

Chassis and cab assembly. The chassis and cab assembly are made from the two pieces of timber (1) and the four pieces of timber (2, 3 and 4). Glue all these pieces together and, when the glue is set, mark out the shape of the cab. On the end of each main frame (1) mark a 45-degree slope, leaving a ½in (12mm) vertical surface for the tailgate to be attached. Cut out the shape of the cab and the main frame with a coping saw or bandsaw.

Mark the centres of the holes for the axles on the main frames ½in (12mm) from the bottom of the frame and 1in (25mm) in from the curves of the cab bottom and the tailgate. Drill ½in (12mm) holes for the axles. When drilling the hole for the rear axle, place a piece of scrap timber between the main frames for support. Drill these holes vertically through the assembly to ensure that the wheels will run smoothly.

DIAGRAM 2

Cut out the four wheels (12) with the hole saw (see Tools, page 11) and two dowels for the axles (6). Insert an axle into one wheel, ensuring that the axle finishes flush with the outside edge of the wheel. When this is done, glue the wheel in position. Repeat this operation for the second axle. Place the pieces of ¼in (6mm) ply (5) square with the back and top of the cab section. Insert an axle and wheel in the hole in the main frame at the cab bottom. Mark the shape of the cab and the wheel on the plywood. Allow ¼in (6mm) clearance around the wheel and cut to shape, (shaded areas in Diagram 2). Glue both pieces in position on the cab sides to simulate mudguards.

The wheels and axles should be put on one side at this stage until the assembly has been painted.

DIAGRAM 3 (see next page)

The body section. Make the body section from the three pieces of timber (7 and 8) and the two pieces of ¼in (6mm) plywood (9). Glue these together to form a box.

When it is assembled, check the internal dimensions of the body to ensure that the bricks will fit into it with a slight clearance.

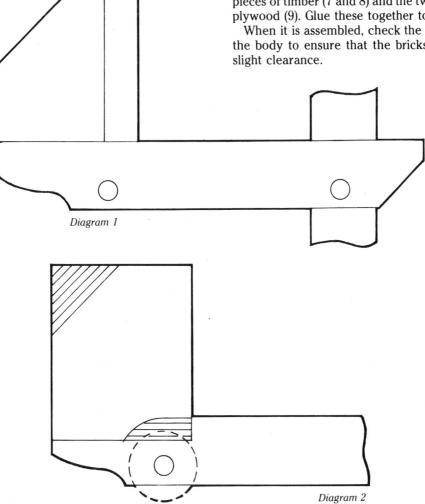

Diagram 1

Diagram 2

DIAGRAM 4

Glue the body on to the mainframe and cab section, allowing an equal overhang at each side. Cut a piece of 3/16in (4mm) plywood (10) to shape for the tailgate by rounding the two bottom corners. This can be cut with a coping saw. Glue this in position on to the mainframes and in line with the body section.

At this stage, it is advisable to paint the whole assembly and the wheels. Ensure that no paint gets into the holes in the mainframes where the axles fit. When dry, the wheels and axles should be inserted into the holes in the mainframe and the second wheels pushed on at the opposite side until the axles are flush with the outside edge. Check that the wheels revolve freely. When this is achieved, remove the two wheels, apply a small amount of glue on the end of the axles, and push the two wheels back into position, with the axle flush with the outside edge of the wheel. Care must be taken when applying the glue to the axle to prevent any coming into contact with the mainframe, and so preventing free movement of the axle.

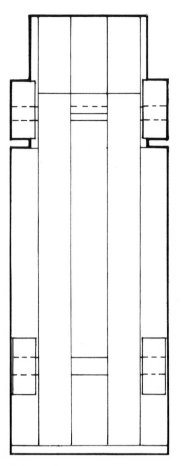

Diagram 4

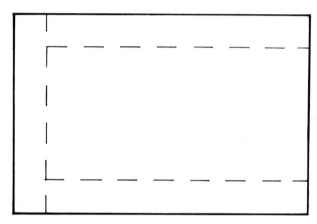

Diagram 3

THE BRICKS

Cut sixteen bricks (11) from $1\frac{7}{8} \times 1\frac{7}{8} \times 1\frac{7}{8}$in (45 × 45 × 45mm) timber, ensuring that they are cubes. Treat each brick with sandpaper, removing sharp edges and corners.

I painted the bricks four different colours, but you can use any number or combination of colours you prefer.

The windows of the cab can either be painted on, or the shapes cut out of black adhesive material and stuck on.

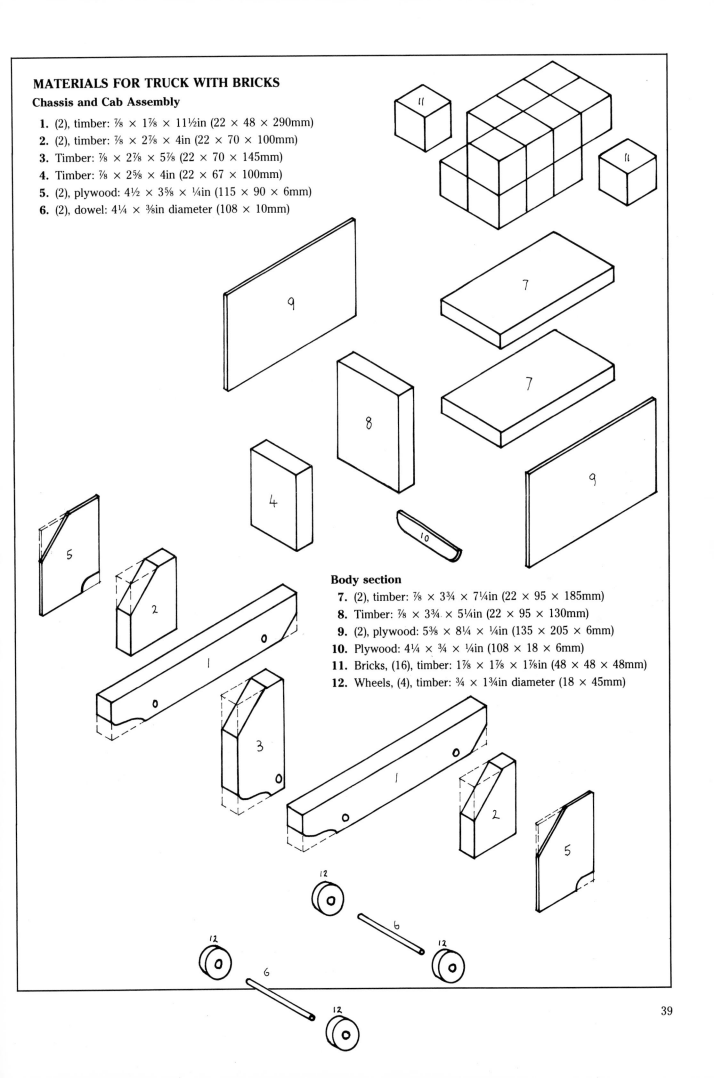

MATERIALS FOR TRUCK WITH BRICKS

Chassis and Cab Assembly

1. (2), timber: ⅞ × 1⅞ × 11½in (22 × 48 × 290mm)

2. (2), timber: ⅞ × 2⅞ × 4in (22 × 70 × 100mm)

3. Timber: ⅞ × 2⅞ × 5⅞ (22 × 70 × 145mm)

4. Timber: ⅞ × 2⅝ × 4in (22 × 67 × 100mm)

5. (2), plywood: 4½ × 3⅝ × ¼in (115 × 90 × 6mm)

6. (2), dowel: 4¼ × ⅜in diameter (108 × 10mm)

Body section

7. (2), timber: ⅞ × 3¾ × 7¼in (22 × 95 × 185mm)

8. Timber: ⅞ × 3¾ × 5¼in (22 × 95 × 130mm)

9. (2), plywood: 5⅜ × 8¼ × ¼in (135 × 205 × 6mm)

10. Plywood: 4¼ × ¾ × ¼in (108 × 18 × 6mm)

11. Bricks, (16), timber: 1⅞ × 1⅞ × 1⅞in (48 × 48 × 48mm)

12. Wheels, (4), timber: ¾ × 1¾in diameter (18 × 45mm)

PULL ALONG TOYS

There is no limit to the types of animal which you can model for these toys. For these two, I have chosen quite substantial timber, as this helps with their stability, but you can use any piece you have available.

Mind yourself, ducky!

Shown here are drawings of the animals I used. Each one is half full-size. Use graph paper to reproduce the drawing to the size you require.

DIAGRAM (see page 42)

Body of toy. Draw out the animal shape you require on graph paper. Cut out the shape and place it on the piece of timber, draw around it, and cut out the shape with a coping saw. If you possess an electric bandsaw, numerous in-

tricate shapes can be cut quickly and accurately. When the shape is cut out, mark and drill the holes for the axles. Ensure that the holes are drilled vertically. The holes should be 1in (25mm) from each end, ½in (12mm) from the bottom and ⅜in (10mm) in diameter. Drill the hole for the pull cord in the centre of the front of the body 1in (25mm) from the bottom and ¼in (6mm) in diameter and to a depth just beyond the axle hole. Then, at right angles to it, drill a ⅜in (10mm) hole in the bottom of the base to join up with it. Enlarge this hole to ⅜in (10mm) and to a

40

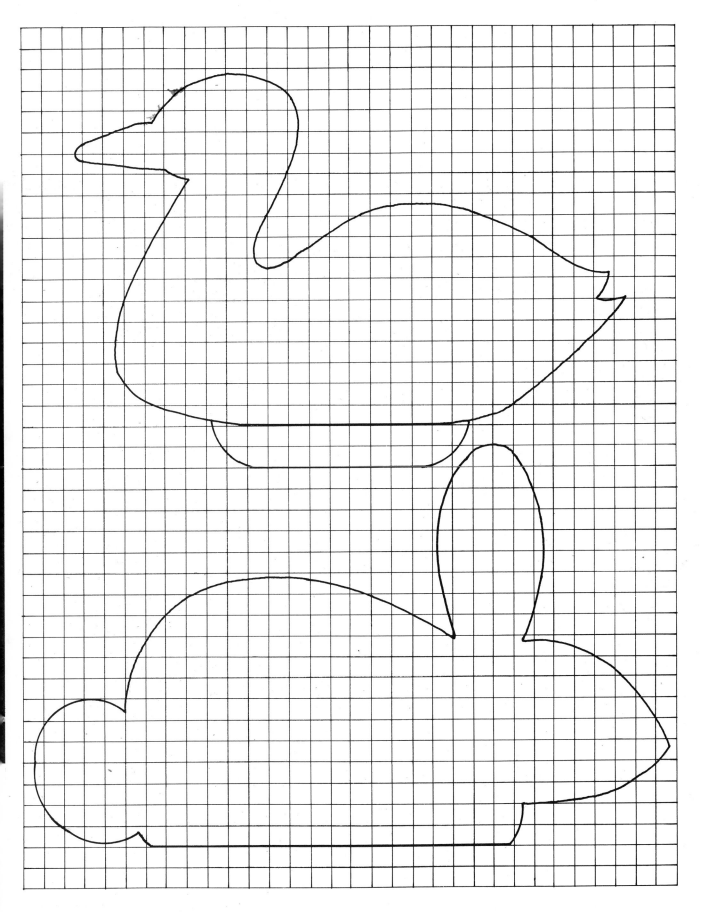

MATERIALS FOR PULL ALONG TOYS

1. Body of toy, timber: 13 × 8 × 1½in (330 × 200 × 37mm)
2. Wheels (4), timber: 2¼ diameter × ⅝in (55 × 15mm)
3. Axle (2), dowel: 2¾ × ⅜in diameter (70 × 10mm)
4. Handle dowel, dowel: 1 × ⅞in diameter (25 × 22mm)
   Length of Cord

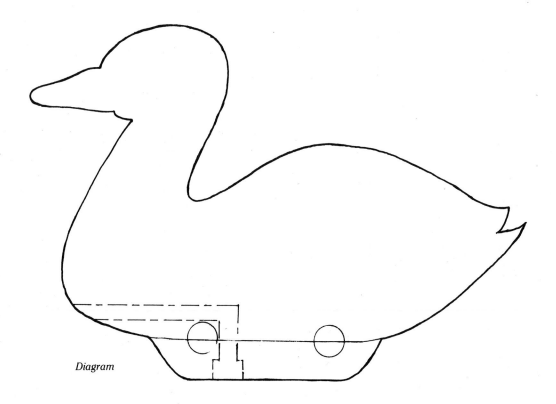

Diagram

depth of ¼in (6mm). This recess will house the cord. Ensure that this hole does not interfere with the axle hole.

With a smoothing plane, chamfer or round off the bottom edges of the body. Cut the four wheels (2) with the hole saw and the two axles to length (3).

Glue one end of an axle in position, with the end flush with the outside edge of the wheel. Insert the wheel in the axle hole and glue the second wheel into position. Ensure the wheels turn freely. Repeat this operation with the second axle. It is advisable to paint the body of the toy before the wheels and axles are finally fitted.

To attach the cord to the toy, insert a piece of soft wire in the hole in the front of the toy and work it through to the base. Tie a double knot in one end of the piece of cord, and fasten the other end to the piece of soft wire. Pull the wire through with the cord attached. The double knot will not allow the cord to be pulled right through and the recess in the hole will hide the knot. For easier grip, cut a length of dowel (4), drill a ¼in (6mm) hole through its centre, and thread the end of the cord through it. Tie a second double knot to prevent the dowel slipping off.

Sand down the body of the toy well and round off all the edges. Depending on what timber you have used, you can either varnish to give a nice wood finish, or paint to the colour of your choice.

HOBBYHORSE

A staunch favourite from Victorian times. With a child's imagination great battles and races can be fought and won.

DIAGRAM 1

Body of horse. In the centre of the handrail (1) and the bottom rail (2), mark and drill out a ⅞in (22mm) diameter hole with a twist bit.

Mark and cut out the shapes for the handles on the handrail with a coping saw and with a spokeshave shape the handles for easier grip.

DIAGRAM 2

In the centre of each end of the bottom rail, drill a ⅞in (22mm) diameter hole for the axles; to a depth of 1½in (37mm).

DIAGRAM 3 (see next page)

Mark and cut out the two wheels (3). In the centre of the wheels drill a 1in (25mm) hole.

Cut the axles (4) to length.

Mark and cut out two 2in (50mm) diameter plywood circles (5).

Glue a circle to the end of each axle, insert the axle through the hole in the wheel, and glue the axle in position in the hole at the end off the bottom rail. Ensure that the wheel turns freely. Repeat this operation for the second wheel.

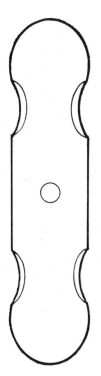

Diagram 1

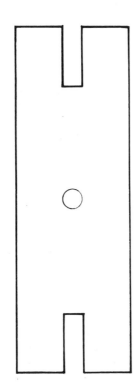

Diagram 2

'I got a hobby horse!'

43

DIAGRAM 4

Insert the body dowel (6) in the hole in the bottom rail. The dowel should protrude 2in (50mm). When this is done glue it into position.

Insert the opposite end of the body dowel in the hole in the handrail until 6in (150mm) protrudes. Glue the handrail in position. Ensure the handrail is in line with the bottom rail. The easiest way to do this is to place both rails on the same flat surface when glueing.

DIAGRAM 5

In the centre of the endpiece (7) drill a ⅞in (22mm) hole. In the opposite end, mark and cut out a groove of the thickness of the wood, to be used for the head and cut to a depth of 2in (50mm). Glue this in position on the end of the body dowel, so that the groove is at right angles to the handrail.

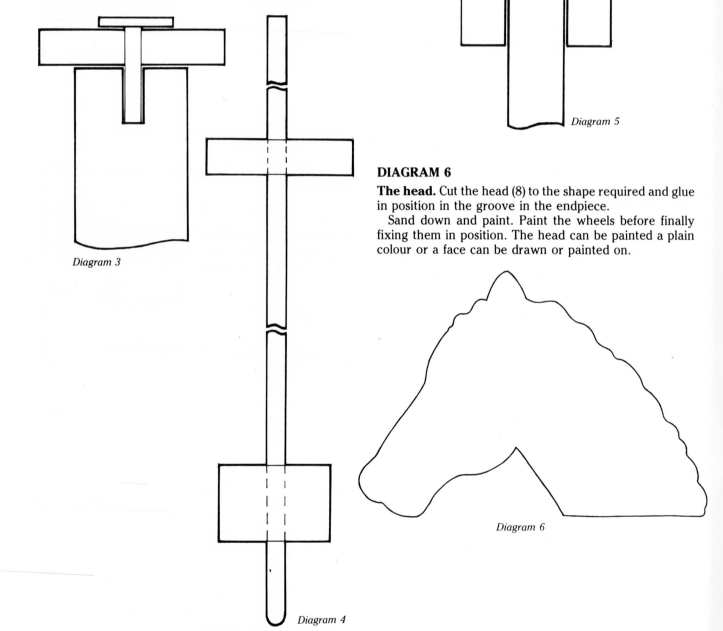

Diagram 3

Diagram 5

DIAGRAM 6

The head. Cut the head (8) to the shape required and glue in position in the groove in the endpiece.

Sand down and paint. Paint the wheels before finally fixing them in position. The head can be painted a plain colour or a face can be drawn or painted on.

Diagram 4

Diagram 6

MATERIALS FOR HOBBYHORSE

1. Handrail, timber: 18 × 4 × ⅞in (457 × 100 × 22mm)
2. Bottom rail, timber: 9 × 3 × 2in (228 × 75 × 50mm)
3. Wheels (2), timber: 5 diameter × ⅞in (125 dia × 22mm)
4. Axles (2), dowel: ⅞ diameter × 2½in (22 dia × 62mm)
5. Plywood (2), plywood: 2 diameter × ¼in (50 × 6mm)
6. Body dowel, dowel: 36 × ⅞in diameter (914 × 22mm)
7. Endpiece, timber: 4 × 4 × 2in (100 × 100 × 50mm)
8. Head, timber: 9 × 6 × ⅞in (228 × 150 × 22mm)

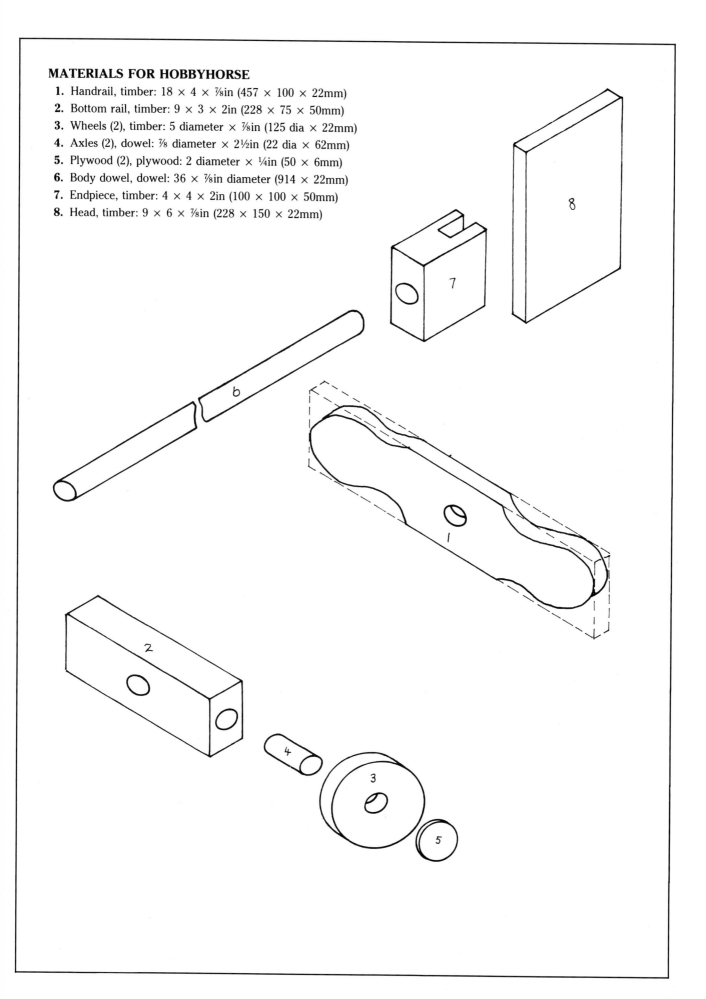

3
GAMES

SKITTLES

The traditional English game of skittles comes in various forms, but this style, without the alleys, is more suitable for the home, and great fun too.

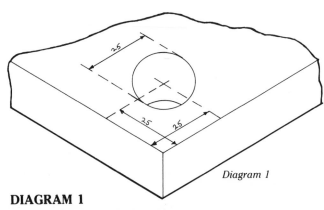

Diagram 1

DIAGRAM 1

Make the base (1) from a piece of ⅞in (22mm) thick chipboard cut into a 12in (300mm) square. Drill a 1in (25mm) diameter hole 1in (25mm) in from one corner. Drill the hole vertically.

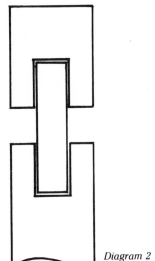

Diagram 2

DIAGRAM 2 (see Materials, page 48)

Take the two posts (2 & 5) and drill a ⅝in (10mm) hole to a depth of ½in (12mm) in the centre of each of the ends. Ensure that the holes are drilled vertically.

Take the dowel for the swivel post (3) and check that it will fit into the two holes. If any difficulty is found ease the dowel by lightly rubbing it down with sandpaper. When the dowel fits into each hole, ensure that there is a ⅜in

Skittle without the alley.

(9mm) gap between the two posts to accommodate the revolving arm. Put the swivel post on one side.

The longer of the two posts (2) can now be fitted into the hole in the base, and glued. The post should finish flush with the underside of the base. Again if difficulty is experienced in fitting it, ease it as before using sandpaper.

DIAGRAM 3

Make the revolving arm (4) from a piece of ¼in (6mm) plywood. To do this, draw two 1in (25mm) diameter circles on the plywood, touching each other, and then draw lines joining the two outside edges of the circles as shown. In the centre of one circle, drill a ½in (12mm) hole and in the centre of the other a ¾in (18mm) hole. When these are drilled, cut out the shape, as shown.

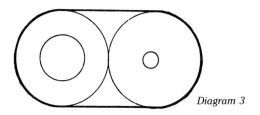

Diagram 3

The swivel post (3) can now be glued into the hole in the top of the post (2). Apply a little glue to the side of the swivel post and push it into the hole. Wipe away any excess glue and, when the glue has dried, fit the revolving arm (4) over the swivel post and ensure that it revolves freely.

Now glue the top part of the post (5) to the swivel post, ensuring that no glue comes into contact with the revolving arm. Again, check that the arm revolves freely. (It is advisable to paint the revolving arm and allow it to dry, before glueing the top of the post (5) into position).

The skittles. Cut the skittles (6) from a ¾in (19mm) diameter dowel. Each skittle is 3in (75mm) long. You require nine.

DIAGRAM 4

The ball (7) is cut from a 2in (50mm) cube, using the hole saw as described in the Tools section (page 11). Secure the cube in a vice, allowing slightly more than half of the cube to protrude above the jaws. Then, using the saw, cut half way through the cube, withdraw the saw, and remove the cube from the vice. Turn the cube upside-down and complete the cutting of the circle. The central drill of the tool will have pierced the cube completely and this hole will enable you to guide the hole saw into position to cut an accurate circle. When this is done, turn the cube through 90° and repeat the operation.

This gives a reasonably shaped ball, with a hole through the centre. Although it is not exactly round it is adequate for the job. The alternative is to purchase a wooden ball.

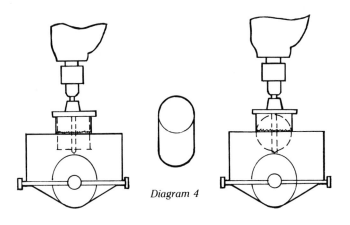

Diagram 4

DIAGRAM 5

Sand down the base, the posts, the skittles and the ball. Then paint them. When everything is painted, mark out the position of the skittles on the base, as shown, and then either paint on circles to the diameter of the skittles or cut out circles of adhesive material to mark the position of the skittles for easy replacement.

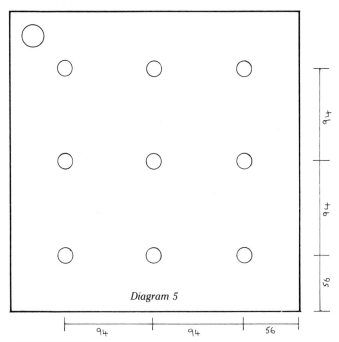

Diagram 5

DIAGRAM 6

Attach the ball to the revolving arm with a length of cord. First, thread the cord through the hole in the ball and knot it. Tie enough knots in the cord so as not to allow it to be pulled through the hole.

Place the ball on the spot marking the skittle furthest from the post, and measure the length of cord required to fasten it to the revolving arm, again threading it through the hole and knotting it as before.

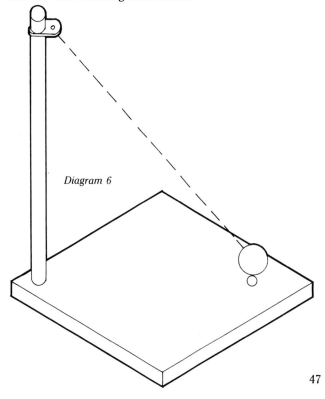

Diagram 6

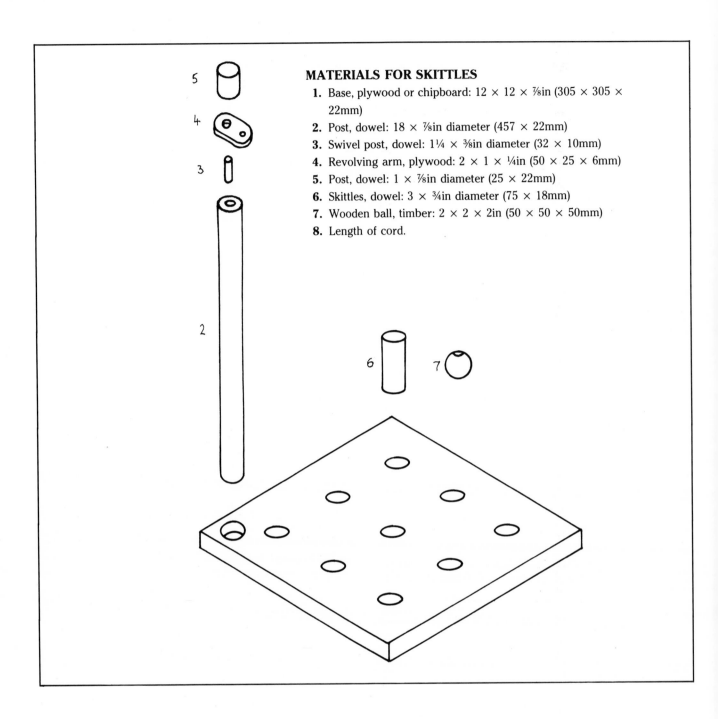

MATERIALS FOR SKITTLES

1. Base, plywood or chipboard: 12 × 12 × ⅞in (305 × 305 × 22mm)
2. Post, dowel: 18 × ⅞in diameter (457 × 22mm)
3. Swivel post, dowel: 1¼ × ⅜in diameter (32 × 10mm)
4. Revolving arm, plywood: 2 × 1 × ¼in (50 × 25 × 6mm)
5. Post, dowel: 1 × ⅞in diameter (25 × 22mm)
6. Skittles, dowel: 3 × ¾in diameter (75 × 18mm)
7. Wooden ball, timber: 2 × 2 × 2in (50 × 50 × 50mm)
8. Length of cord.

DRAUGHTSBOARD

Nearly every household possesses a draughts or chess board. This particular design will appeal to children and parents alike because it is unusual. It is relatively simple to construct and, with the addition of a set of chessmen, the toy could become a permanent feature in any living room or children's room. To complete the toy, use brass fittings which will greatly enhance its appearance.

Portable draughts (or chess) board — huff, puff and check.

DIAGRAM 1 (see page 52)

Side A. (*See next page.*) Glue the five pieces of timber (1 and 2) to the first plywood sides (3). When dry, glue the second side (3) in position on the framework, ensuring that

the framework is square and flush with the edges of the plywood sides.

Mark and cut out the handle (6) with a coping saw. Cut the handle from one piece of timber and then cut the shape in half. This will ensure that both halves of the handles are the same shape. On the ends of the four surround pieces (4, 5) cut mitres and glue these in position

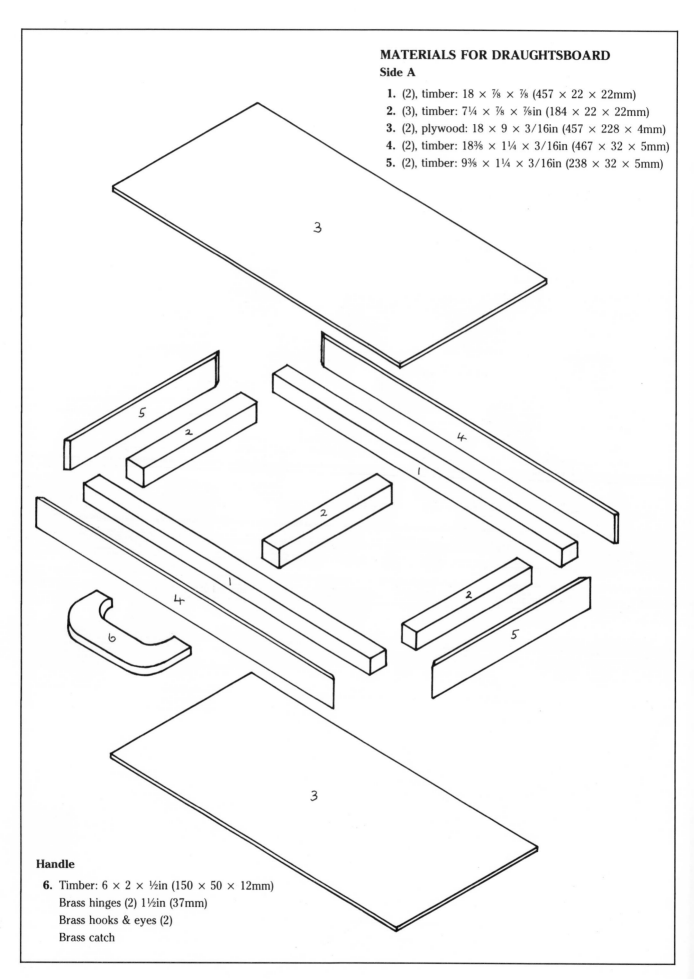

MATERIALS FOR DRAUGHTSBOARD
Side A

1. (2), timber: 18 × ⅞ × ⅞ (457 × 22 × 22mm)
2. (3), timber: 7¼ × ⅞ × ⅞in (184 × 22 × 22mm)
3. (2), plywood: 18 × 9 × 3/16in (457 × 228 × 4mm)
4. (2), timber: 18⅜ × 1¼ × 3/16in (467 × 32 × 5mm)
5. (2), timber: 9⅜ × 1¼ × 3/16in (238 × 32 × 5mm)

Handle

6. Timber: 6 × 2 × ½in (150 × 50 × 12mm)
   Brass hinges (2) 1½in (37mm)
   Brass hooks & eyes (2)
   Brass catch

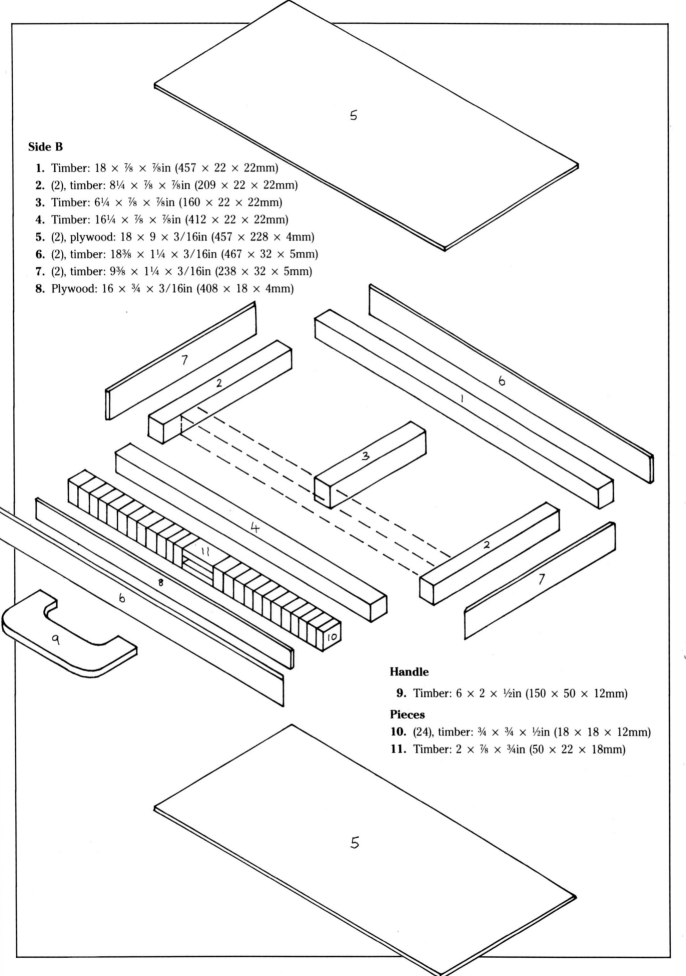

Side B

1. Timber: $18 \times \frac{7}{8} \times \frac{7}{8}$in ($457 \times 22 \times 22$mm)
2. (2), timber: $8\frac{1}{4} \times \frac{7}{8} \times \frac{7}{8}$in ($209 \times 22 \times 22$mm)
3. Timber: $6\frac{1}{4} \times \frac{7}{8} \times \frac{7}{8}$in ($160 \times 22 \times 22$mm)
4. Timber: $16\frac{1}{4} \times \frac{7}{8} \times \frac{7}{8}$in ($412 \times 22 \times 22$mm)
5. (2), plywood: $18 \times 9 \times 3/16$in ($457 \times 228 \times 4$mm)
6. (2), timber: $18\frac{3}{8} \times 1\frac{1}{4} \times 3/16$in ($467 \times 32 \times 5$mm)
7. (2), timber: $9\frac{3}{8} \times 1\frac{1}{4} \times 3/16$in ($238 \times 32 \times 5$mm)
8. Plywood: $16 \times \frac{3}{4} \times 3/16$in ($408 \times 18 \times 4$mm)

Handle

9. Timber: $6 \times 2 \times \frac{1}{2}$in ($150 \times 50 \times 12$mm)

Pieces

10. (24), timber: $\frac{3}{4} \times \frac{3}{4} \times \frac{1}{2}$in ($18 \times 18 \times 12$mm)
11. Timber: $2 \times \frac{7}{8} \times \frac{3}{4}$in ($50 \times 22 \times 18$mm)

around the side. Before glueing one of the longer sides in position, glue and screw one half of the handle in position, flush with one edge.

DIAGRAM 2

Side B. Glue the five pieces of timber (1, 2, 3, 4) to the plywood side (5). The piece of timber (4) is positioned so as to form a 1in (25mm) recess.

Glue the second side (5) in position. Again ensure that the framework is square. On the ends of the four side-pieces (6, 7) cut mitres and glue three of them in position on the edges of the framework, leaving the recess open.

DIAGRAM 3

Glue the piece of plywood (8) to the underside of the remaining side-piece and check that it is central.

Check that this side-piece fits into the recess and completes the framework.

Glue the timber block (11) in position in the recess and screw the catch in position in the centre. Screw the other part of the catch in position on the detachable side-piece and check that two will fit together.

DIAGRAM 4

The two sides should now be joined together. Mark out and, with a chisel, cut the recesses for the two hinges on both sides. The hinges must be flush with the edging strip. Screw the hinges in position. Ensure that, when the two sides are folded together, the edges are flush.

DIAGRAM 5

With the two halves folded together, mark the position for the second half of the handle on the detachable top-piece. Glue and screw the handle in position. Fix the two metal catches in position at either side of the handle.

Cut the twenty-four draughts pieces (10) to size.

To sand down and paint, it is advisable to separate the two halves and the top piece. The squares can either be painted on, or cut from adhesive paper and stuck in position. Paint the draught pieces in contrasting colours.

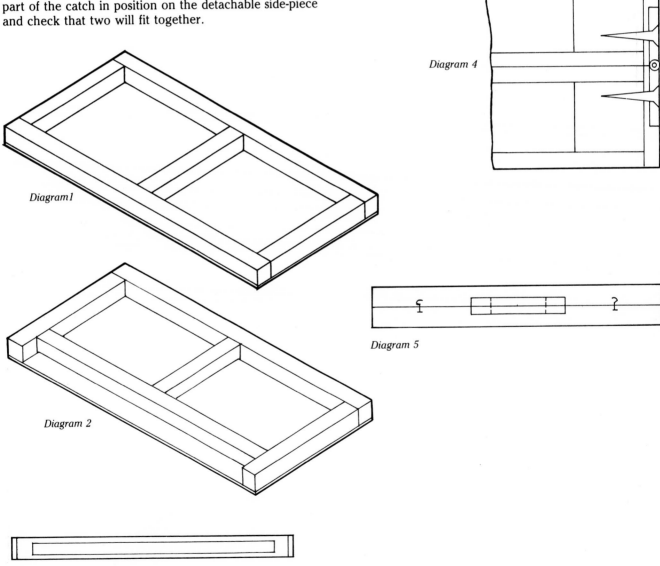

Diagram 1

Diagram 2

Diagram 3

Diagram 4

Diagram 5

HOOPLA

This game will give children lots of enjoyment as they challenge each other for the highest score. I have used rubber rings for the hoops as they are less noisy and will not damage the backboard. The box on the base should collect the rings which miss the target, and stop them rolling away under the furniture etc.

DIAGRAM 1

On the backboard (1) mark out the centres for the pegs (2). See Materials on page 54.

DIAGRAM 2

Drill out the holes for the pegs with a twist drill at an angle of 45 degrees. The holes should have the same diameter as the pegs (for drilling instructions, see Boat, page 18).

Cut the nine pieces of dowel for the pegs, and glue them in position in the holes. Ensure that all the pegs are at the same angle and protrude all the way through the backboard. When the glue has set, use a smoothing plane to plane the ends of the pegs level with the backboard.

DIAGRAM 3

Base. Glue and screw the base (3) to the backboard. Glue and screw the two side panels (4) and front panel (5) to the base to form the box.

Sand down the whole assembly and paint it in the colours of your choice. Paint the pegs a contrasting colour to the backboard, and either paint or stick on numbers of differing values under each peg. For the hoops use 2in (50mm) rubber rings, or alternatively wooden rings.

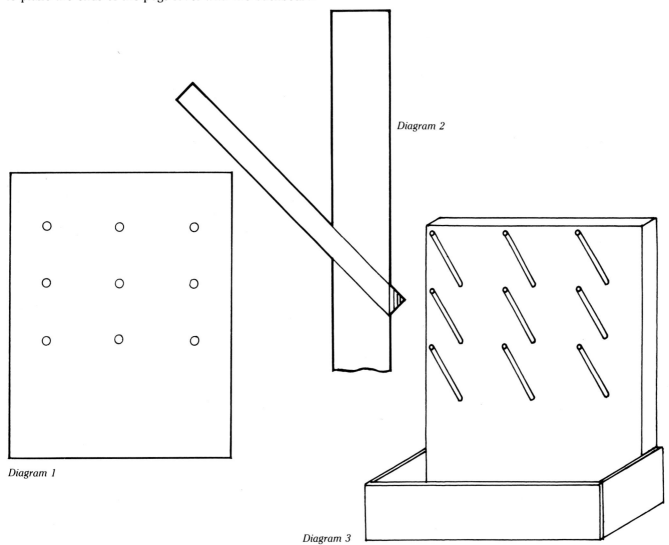

Diagram 2

Diagram 1

Diagram 3

53

MATERIALS FOR HOOPLA

1. Backboard, plywood/chipboard: 12 × 15 × ¾in (305 × 375 × 18mm)
2. Pegs (9), dowel: 3½ × ⅜in diameter (87 × 10mm)
3. Base, timber: 12 × 3 × ¾in (305 × 75 × 18mm)
4. Box side panels (2), plywood: 3¾ × 3 × ¼in (93 × 75 × 6mm)
5. Box front, plywood: 12½ × 3 × ¼in (317 × 75 × 6mm)
6. Optional wooden rings (6): 2 × ⅛in diameter (50 × 2mm)

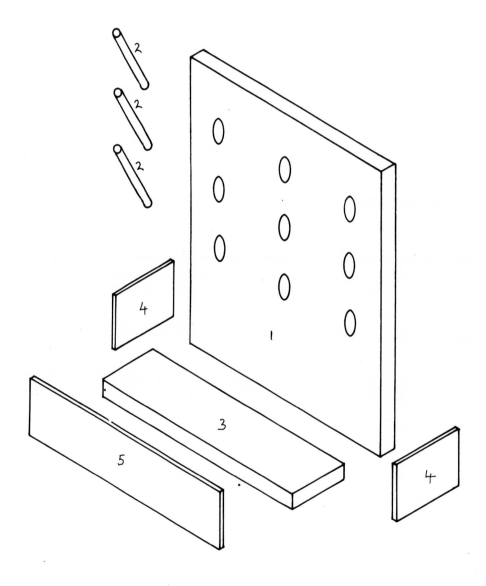

Hooked on hoopla.

SOLITAIRE

Solitaire is an old and basically very simple game, and it is still popular with children. Playing the game alone, or with a partner, a child can be happily occupied for hours.

All for one, and one for all.

DIAGRAM 1

Cut the base (1) into a square. Mark the holes for the pegs and drill out to a depth of ½in (12mm). Ensure that the holes are drilled vertically. With a smoothing plane, round off all the edges of the base. An electric drill, fitted into a drill stand, will enable you to perform the drilling quickly and accurately, but it can also be done with a hand drill. If you only have a hand drill, then, because of the thickness of the pegs, you will have to drill a ¼in (6mm) hole first, and then enlarge this to ½in (12mm). Using an ordinary twist drill will leave the bottom of the holes rounded.

DIAGRAM 2

Cut the thirty-two pegs (2) from ⅜in (10mm) dowel 1in (25mm) in length, and, so that they will sit neatly in the holes, round off one end of the pegs, using sandpaper.

If you have an electric drill mounted on a stand, this will be of great assistance. Lightly clamp each peg in the drill and, as it revolves, hold the sandpaper to it at an angle, equal to that of the bottom of the hole.

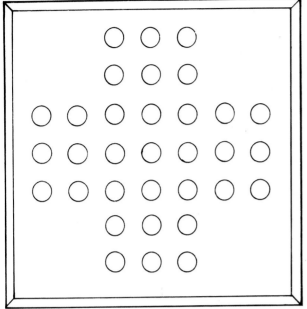

Diagram 1

DIAGRAM 3

After sanding, the base can be either painted or varnished, and the pegs painted a contrasting colour. Painting the pegs can be a rather messy and tedious job. To avoid too many fingermarks and painted fingers, take a piece of scrap plywood and at 1in (25mm) intervals, hammer ¾in (22mm) long panel pins through it, so that they stick out at the other side. Do this with as many panel pins as the piece of plywood will allow.

Next, with great care, turn the plywood over and place it on a firm base. Take a peg and put it on top of one of the panel pin tips, and, with the rounded end at the bottom, lightly hammer it until it is firmly in position. Repeat this operation with as many pegs as you can. This will enable you to paint the pegs without too much mess.

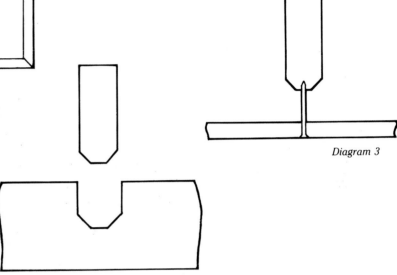

Diagram 2

Diagram 3

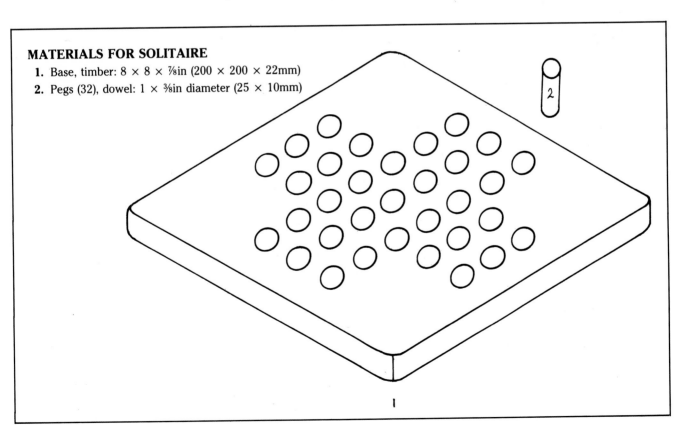

MATERIALS FOR SOLITAIRE

1. Base, timber: 8 × 8 × ⅞in (200 × 200 × 22mm)
2. Pegs (32), dowel: 1 × ⅜in diameter (25 × 10mm)

HAMMER AND PEGS

These types of toy have always been popular with younger children, for they can hammer away, and not get into trouble! It is an easy toy to make, in a number of ways and with varying numbers and sizes of pegs and hammers. Described here are two different methods:

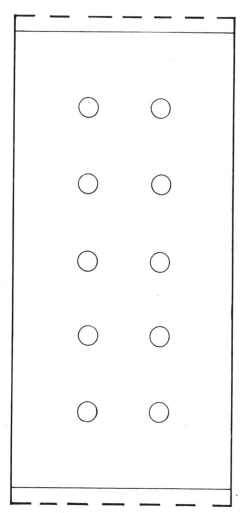

Diagram 1A

Banging in pegs. Bang on.

DIAGRAM 1(A)

METHOD A. Take the centre section of the frame (1) and decide how many pegs you wish to have. In the case of 'A, I have used ten. Mark out the centres of the holes for the pegs, equal distances apart, making allowances for the joints at each end, and drill out the holes with a twistbit, taking care not to split the wood, and ensuring that the holes are drilled vertically.

DIAGRAM 2(A)

In the centre of the two end-support pieces (2) mark out a channel to the thickness of the centre section, and to a depth of ⅜in (10mm). With a tenon saw, cut along the lines to the required depth and remove the waste wood with a chisel, leaving the bottom of the channel level. When sawing, keep the saw cut to the wasteside of the marked lines to ensure a neat tight joint. When both channels have been cut out, fit and glue the centre section in position, ensuring that the end support pieces are at right angles to it.

Cut the required number of pegs (3) to length.

In both versions A and B, ensure that the pegs are cut to a length of not more than half the height of the side pieces, so that when the pegs are hammered in flush with the centre section, the opposite end will not protrude beyond the bottom of the end section. This will prevent any damage to the surface on which the toy is standing. (*Instructions follow on page 62.*)

Diagram 2A

MATERIALS FOR HAMMER AND PEGS

METHOD A

1. Centre section, timber: $\frac{7}{8} \times 6 \times 12$in ($22 \times 150 \times 305$mm)
2. End supports (2), timber: $\frac{7}{8} \times 6 \times 6$in ($22 \times 150 \times 150$mm)
3. Pegs (10), dowel: $3\frac{1}{2} \times \frac{1}{2}$in diameter ($87 \times 12$mm)
4. Mallet head, timber hardwood: $1 \times 2 \times 2\frac{1}{2}$in ($25 \times 50 \times 64$mm)
5. Mallet shaft, dowel: $6\frac{1}{2} \times \frac{7}{8}$in ($165 \times 22$mm)

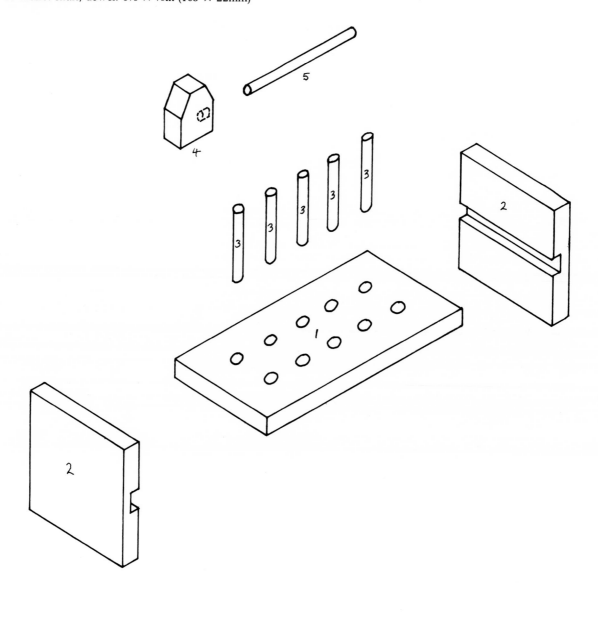

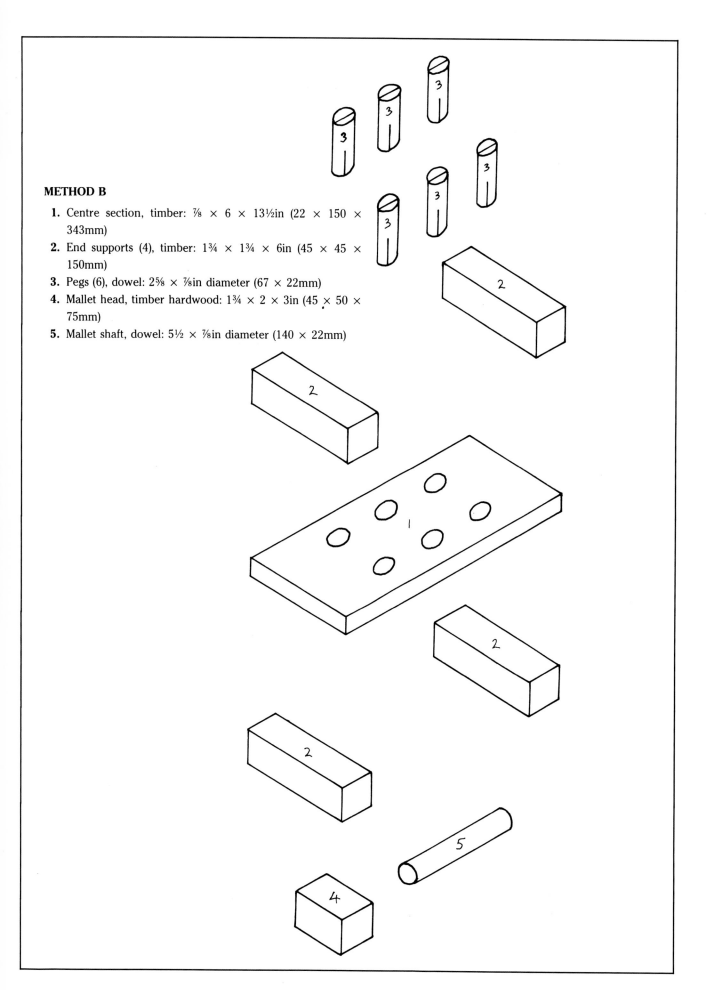

METHOD B

1. Centre section, timber: ⅞ × 6 × 13½in (22 × 150 × 343mm)
2. End supports (4), timber: 1¾ × 1¾ × 6in (45 × 45 × 150mm)
3. Pegs (6), dowel: 2⅝ × ⅞in diameter (67 × 22mm)
4. Mallet head, timber hardwood: 1¾ × 2 × 3in (45 × 50 × 75mm)
5. Mallet shaft, dowel: 5½ × ⅞in diameter (140 × 22mm)

DIAGRAM 3(A)

Make the mallet head (4) from a piece of hardwood. Hardwood is more durable than softwood, and the surface will withstand the rigours of hammering better. In the centre of the mallet head, drill a hole to a depth of ½in (12mm), the diameter of the dowel to be used for the shaft (5). Apply some glue to the end of the shaft and push the shaft into the hole in the mallet head. Ensure that the shaft is at right angles to the head.

DIAGRAM 1(B)

METHOD B. On the centre section (1) mark the required number of holes for the dowels. In this version I use six pegs. Cut out these holes as before: see Diagram 1A, Method A. The end-sections are made up of the timber pieces (2) which are glued to the centre section.

DIAGRAM 2(B)

In this version, I used 1in (25mm) diameter dowels (3). Make a saw cut in the centre of the dowel, three-quarters of its length. In the other end of the dowel, at right angles to the first cut, make another saw cut, again three-quarters of its length. This will enable the pegs to be hammered through the holes more easily.

In this version, due to the extra thickness of the pegs, make a mallet similar to (A), but with a larger head and shaft (4 and 5), to cope with the size of the pegs.

I finished both these versions with a clear varnish rather than with paint, to eliminate the problem of the holes becoming clogged. When dry, the pegs will pass through the holes with just a slight tapping of the mallet.

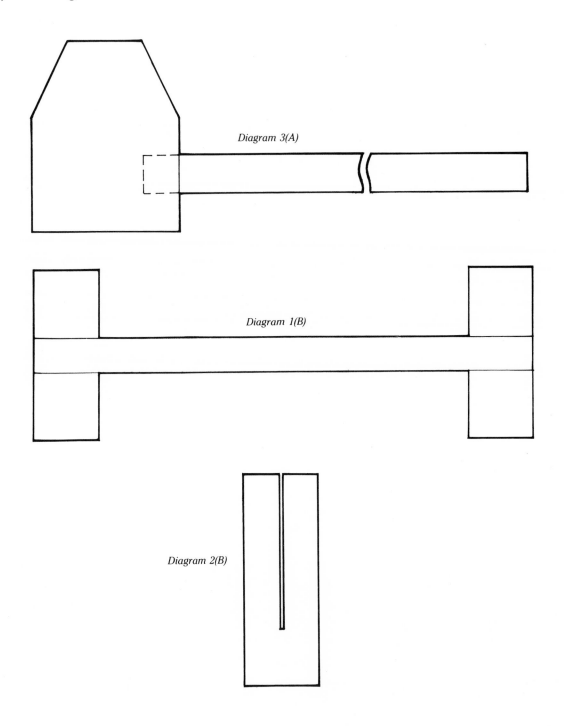

Diagram 3(A)

Diagram 1(B)

Diagram 2(B)

4
LARGER TOYS

EASEL AND BLACKBOARD

An easel and blackboard are among the first toys required for any playroom or child's room. Apart from the enjoyment of chalking on the board, it gives a child some insight into what to expect when school age is reached.

DIAGRAM 1

With this easel design I have splayed the legs to give extra stability. This makes the mortice and tenon joint a little more difficult to construct, but the finished effect is pleasing. You will require two steel flap hinges and a length of plastic cable to complete the easel.

Easel. Mark out the angles with a sliding bevel on the ends of both bottom (1) and top rails (2). Allow 1in (25mm) on each end for the tenon and cut to length.

DIAGRAM 2 (see Materials, page 66)

With a mortice marking gauge, mark out the tenons on the ends of the rails to a depth of 1in (25mm). The tenon should be one-third the thickness of the timber. Cut out the tenons with a tenon saw and cut a ½in (12mm) shoulder on the top of each tenon.

If required, mark out the curved shape on the top rail and cut it out with a coping saw. You can make the shape as elaborate as you require. If you do decide to shape the top rail, clamp both rails together and cut out.

DIAGRAM 3

At 3in (75mm) and 19½in (487mm) from the top of each leg, mark out the mortice holes to the width of each tenon. Cut out the mortice holes to the depth of the tenons. Because the legs are splayed, you are cutting the mortice holes to allow for this.

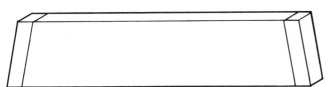

Diagram 1

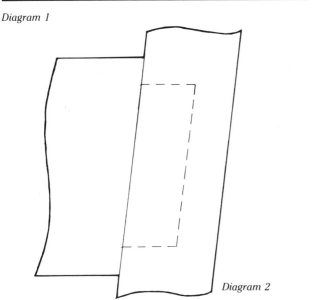

Diagram 2

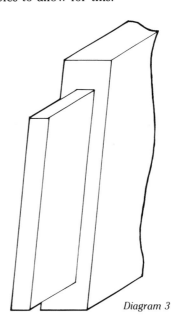

Diagram 3

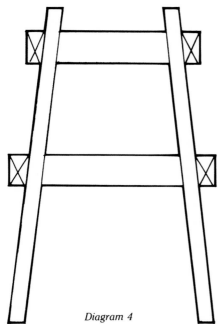

Diagram 4

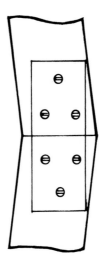

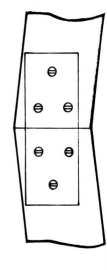

Diagram 6

DIAGRAM 4

When all the joints have been cut, assemble the framework and check that the joints fit correctly. Also check the framework by measuring the internal diagonal measurements. When this is correct, glue and clamp the framework together with sash clamps. When clamping together, the scrap pieces of wood used to protect the framework should be wedge-shaped to allow even pressure to be applied.

DIAGRAM 6

Repeat the whole operation for the other side of the easel. When both sides are completed, join the two frameworks together with steel flap hinges. Lay the two sections flat with the outside faces down and the tops of both legs touching each other. Screw the hinges in position. Ensure that the hinges do not overlap the edges of the legs. Check that, when folded, the two frameworks fit together with the outside edges flush.

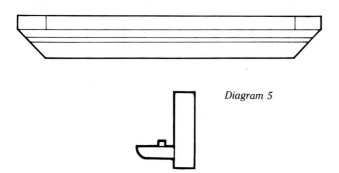

Diagram 5

DIAGRAM 5

Cut the ends of the legs to the correct angles. Do this by setting a sliding bevel to the angle formed between the leg and the rails. Mark this angle on the end of each leg and cut out with a tenon saw. Cut the blackboard support (4) to length. On each end cut a 45-degree angle and with a smoothing plane, round off the outside edges. Glue and screw this to the framework ½in (12mm) from the bottom of the bottom rail. Cut the guide piece (5) to length, and also cut 45-degree angles on each end. Glue this in position on the support piece, allowing for the thickness of the blackboard to be used.

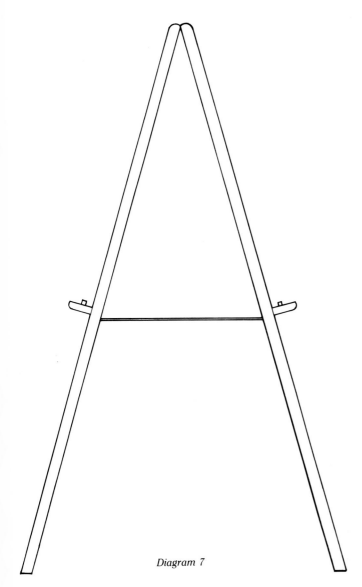

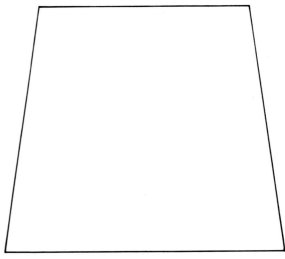

Diagram 8

DIAGRAM 8

Blackboards. Cut the chipboard panels (6) for the blackboard to fit on to the framework and behind the guide pieces.

Sand down and paint the two sections of the easel, preferably in a bright colour to contrast with the blackboards. Choose a plastic cable to match the colour of the easel. Paint the two blackboards with blackboard paint to give a dull matt finish. Alternatively, one board can be painted black and the other a different colour.

Diagram 7

DIAGRAM 7

On the bottom rails 3in (75mm) in from the edge of the leg, underneath the blackboard support, drill 3/16in (4mm) holes.

Thread the plastic cable through all four holes, and tie together in between the two frameworks. Cut the cable long enough to allow the two frameworks to separate a distance of 12in (300mm) at the bottom rail level.

MATERIALS FOR EASEL AND BLACKBOARD
Easel

1. Bottom rail (2): 21¾ × 4 × ⅞in (552 × 101 × 22mm) timber

2. Top rail (2), timber: 17 × 4 × ⅞in (432 × 101 × 22mm)

3. Legs (4), timber: 42 × 1¾ × ⅞in (1067 × 45 × 22mm)

4. Blackboard support (2), timber: 23 × 1¾ × ⅝in (585 × 45 × 15mm)

5. Guide (2), timber: 21½ × 5/16 × 5/16in (545 × 7 × 7mm)

Blackboards

6. Blackboards (2), chipboard: 21½ × 18 × ½in (545 × 457 × 12mm)

Flap hinges (2): 1½ × 2in (37 × 50mm)

Length of plastic

Coated cord

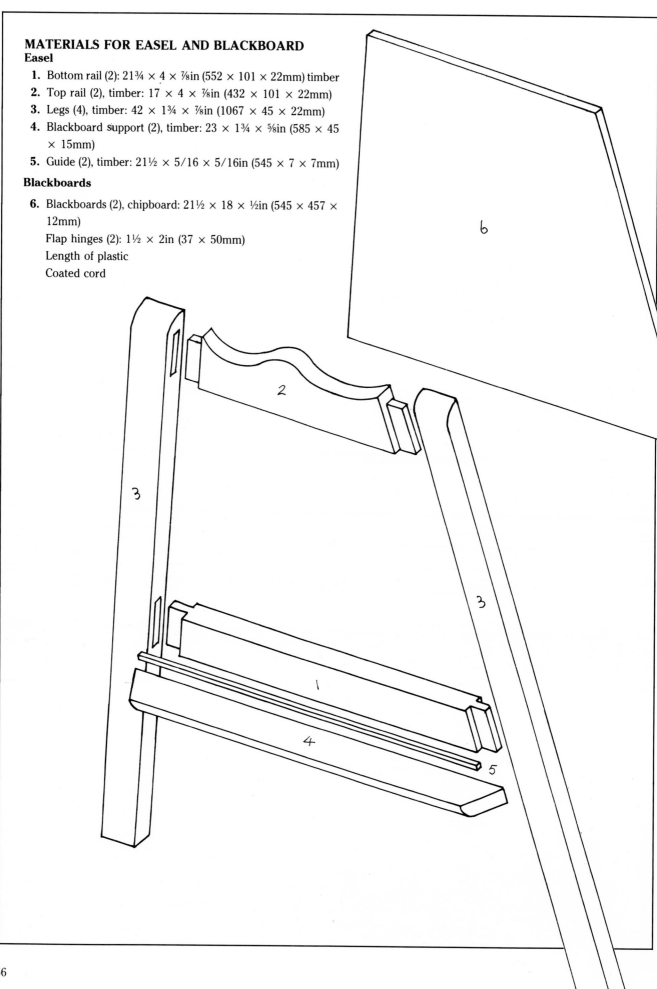

Blackboard. Easel does it!

CASTLE

This castle will bring children hours of pleasure as they enact their make-believe medieval battles. All the sections of the castle are detachable and will pack away neatly into the base. A length of thin cord is required for the lifting of the portcullis.

Castle. Medieval make-believe.

DIAGRAM 1

Base. Cut the two side pieces (1) to shape with a 60-degree slope on each end. Cut the end-pieces to length (2). Glue the two sides and ends together. When dry, remove with a smoothing plane the edges of the end-pieces which protrude beyond the side pieces.

Ensure the assembly sits flat. Cut the plywood top (3) to size and glue it in position on the base.

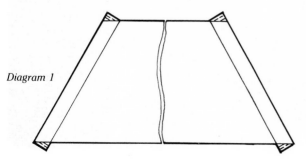

Diagram 1

DIAGRAM 2 (see opposite page, top left)

Towers. All seven towers are constructed in the same way but they vary in height. The four corner towers are the same height, the two front ones are the same as each other, and the rear tower is the tallest.

Cut the four sides (4 & 5) and the three timber squares (6) to size. Two of the squares are used to form the tower and the third is glued on to the base. The tower is then slotted over the square. Glue the four sides to the two timber squares. Ensure that the square at the top of the tower is flush with the top of the sides, and that the bottom square is 1in (25mm) from the bottom.

The third timber square is glued in position on the base. Ensure the square is ¼in (6mm) from the edge and that the tower fits tightly over the top of it.

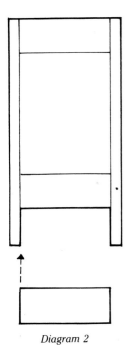

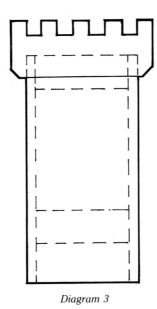

DIAGRAM 3

On the pieces of timber (7-8) mark out the battlements. Make the recesses for the battlements equal. Cut out the recess by either cutting down the lines with a tenon saw and removing the waste with a chisel, or cutting it out with a coping saw. When it has been cut out, glue the four sides together. Ensure that the assembly fits over the tower. Chamfer or round off the bottom edges of the battlements with a smoothing plane.

Glue the battlements on to the top of the tower with ½in (12mm) overlap.

Diagram 3

Diagram 2

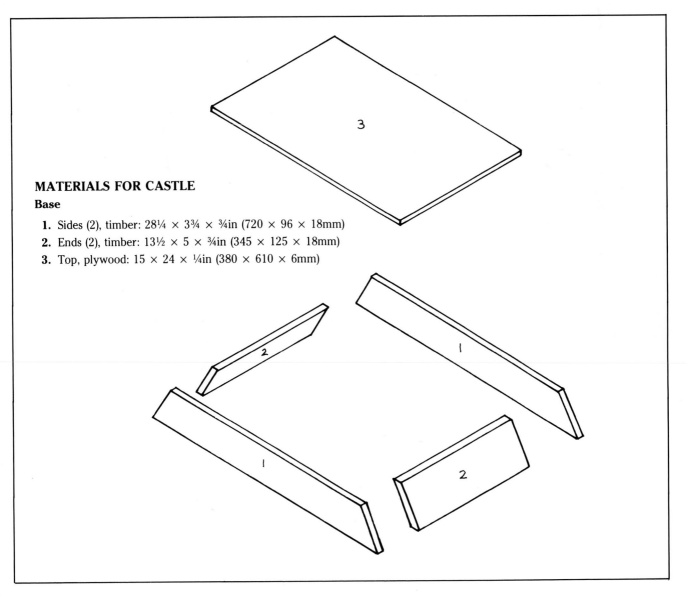

MATERIALS FOR CASTLE
Base

1. Sides (2), timber: 28¼ × 3¾ × ¾in (720 × 96 × 18mm)
2. Ends (2), timber: 13½ × 5 × ¾in (345 × 125 × 18mm)
3. Top, plywood: 15 × 24 × ¼in (380 × 610 × 6mm)

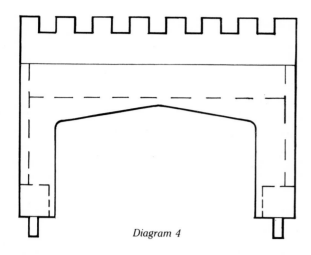

Diagram 4

DIAGRAM 4

Rear compartments (page 72). Mark and cut out the openings on the two plywood front pieces (9). Clamp both pieces together and cut out with a coping saw to ensure both openings are identical.

Cut to size the back (10), the top (11), the two ends (12), and two bottom supports (13), and glue together. Cut the piece of timber for the battlements (15) and mark and cut out the recesses. Glue this in position on the back outside edge flush with the rear wall.

Diagram 5

DIAGRAM 5

In the centre of the two bottom supports, drill ⅜in (10mm) holes to a depth of ¼in (6mm) and glue in the two locating dowels (14). Repeat this operation for both back compartments.

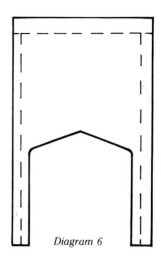

Diagram 6

DIAGRAM 6

Gatehouse (see page 73). Mark and cut out the openings in the front and rear plywood pieces (16). As with the rear compartments clamp both together when cutting out.

Cut the top (18) and the two sides (17). Glue the assembly together.

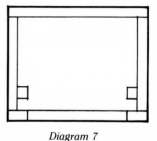

Diagram 7

DIAGRAM 7

Cut the two guides (19) for the portcullis and glue them in position inside the gatehouse assembly.

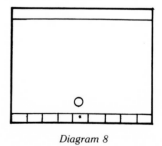

Diagram 8

DIAGRAM 8

Cut the individual blocks (20) for the battlements and glue in position on the front edge. Leave the central piece loose and drill a 1/16in (1mm) hole through the centre of it. This piece is used for lifting the portcullis hole. Drill a 1/16in (1mm) hole as close to the edge of the top as possible. This hole is for the lifting cord to pass through.

Drill a ¼in (6mm) hole in the centre of the top and glue the dowel pieces (21) in position for the flagpole. Ensure the end is flush with the underside of the top.

Battlement Sections

a) Corner towers

4. Sides (8), plywood: $3 \times 6 \times \frac{1}{4}$in ($75 \times 150 \times 6$mm)
5. Sides (8), plywood: $2\frac{1}{2} \times 6 \times \frac{1}{4}$in ($64 \times 150 \times 6$mm)
6. Squares (12), timber: $2\frac{1}{2} \times 2\frac{1}{2} \times \frac{7}{8}$in ($64 \times 64 \times 22$mm)

b) Front central towers

Sides (4), plywood: $3 \times 7 \times \frac{1}{4}$in ($75 \times 178 \times 6$mm)
Sides (4), plywood: $2\frac{1}{2} \times 7 \times \frac{1}{4}$in ($64 \times 178 \times 6$mm)
Squares (6), timber: $2\frac{1}{2} \times 2\frac{1}{2} \times \frac{7}{8}$in ($64 \times 64 \times 22$mm)

c) Rear tower

Sides (2), plywood: $3 \times 8 \times \frac{1}{4}$in ($75 \times 200 \times 6$mm)
Sides (2), plywood: $2\frac{1}{2} \times 8 \times \frac{1}{4}$in ($64 \times 200 \times 6$mm)
Squares (3), timber: $2\frac{1}{2} \times 2\frac{1}{2} \times \frac{7}{8}$in ($64 \times 64 \times 22$mm)

7. Battlements (14), timber: $3\frac{3}{4} \times 1\frac{3}{8} \times \frac{3}{8}$in ($93 \times 35 \times 10$mm)
8. (14), timber: $3 \times 1\frac{3}{8} \times \frac{3}{8}$in ($75 \times 35 \times 10$mm)

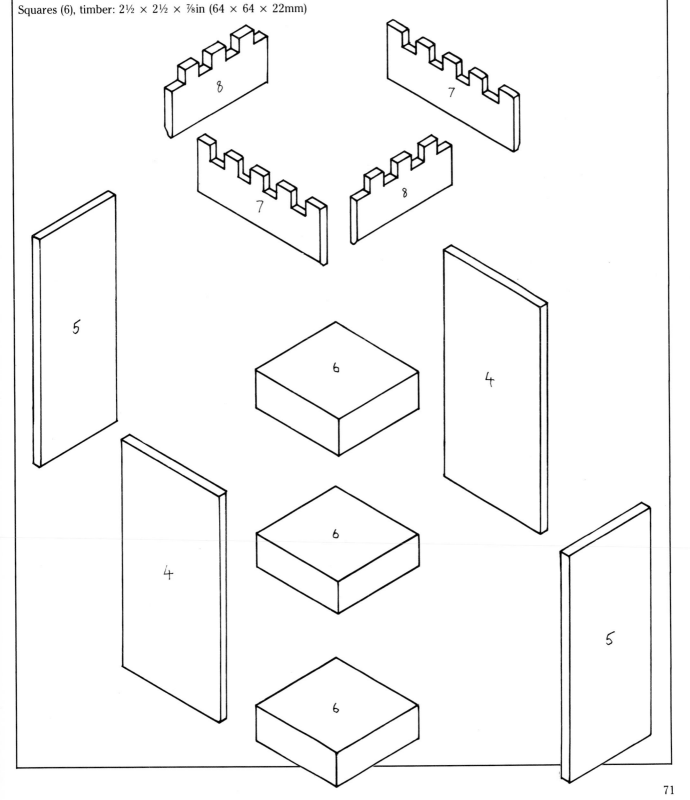

71

Rear compartments

9. Front (2), plywood: 7½ × 4 × ¼in (190 × 100 × 6mm)
10. Back (2), plywood: 7½ × 4 × ¼in (190 × 100 × 6mm)
11. Top, timber: 7 × 2½ × ⅞in (178 × 64 × 22mm)
12. Ends (4), plywood: 3⅛ × 2½ × ¼in (80 × 64 × 6mm)
13. Bottom, timber support (4): 2½ × ⅞ × ⅞in (64 × 22 × 22mm)
14. Dowel (4): 1 × ⅜in diameter (25 × 10mm)
15. Battlements (2), timber: 7½ × 1⅜ × 1⅜in (190 × 35 × 35mm)

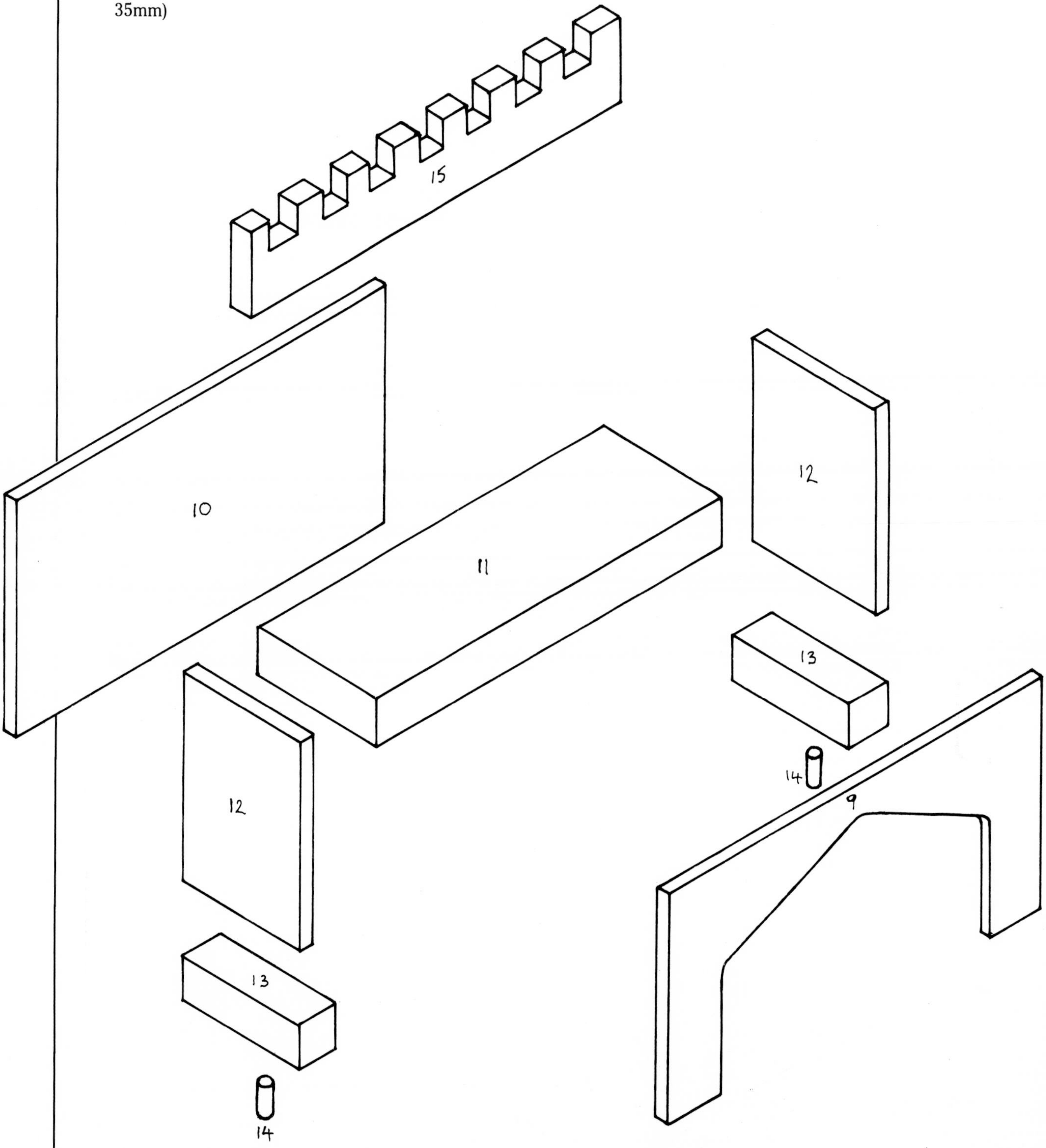

Gatehouse

16. Front and rear (2), plywood: 5⅞ × 3¾ × ¼in (147 × 96 × 6mm)

17. Sides (2), plywood: 5½ × 2½ × ¼in (137 × 64 × 6mm)

18. Top, timber: 3¾ × 2½ × ⅜in (96 × 64 × 10mm)

19. Guides (2), timber: 5 × ⅜ × ⅜in (125 × 10 × 10mm)

19a. Guides (2), timber: 1¾ × 5/16 × 5/16in (43 × 9 × 9mm)

20. Battlements (5), timber: ⅜ × ⅜ × ⅜in (10 × 10 × 10mm)

21. Flagpole, dowel: 4¼ × ¼in diameter (106 × 6mm)

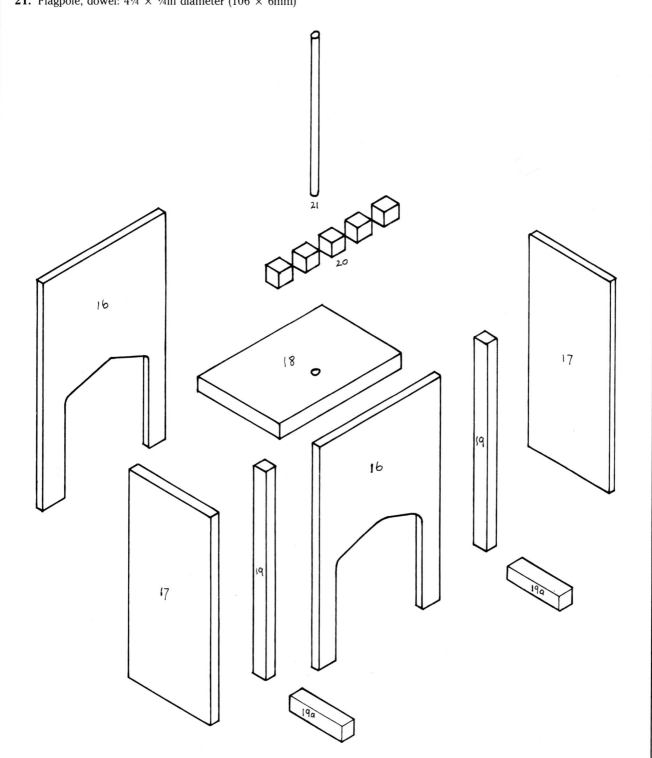

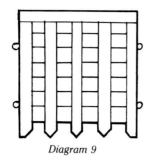
Diagram 9

DIAGRAM 9

Portcullis. Cut the pieces of timber for the portcullis (22, 23, 24) and glue together. To do this place a piece of newspaper or tissue paper on a scrap piece of timber approx. 6in (150mm) square. Knock in two 1in (25mm) panel pins in line, on one side, leaving ½in (12mm) protruding.

On the five upright pieces of the portcullis mark out the positions of the small cross pieces. Place the outside upright against the two panel pins. Place a drop of glue on each end of the cross-pieces and glue them in position on the upright. Repeat this until all pieces are glued together. When the last upright piece is in place, knock in two more panel pins to hold the assembly firm. Ensure the assembly is square, and glue the top piece of the portcullis in position.

Remove any surplus glue from the top surface. When the assembly is dry, remove it from the panel pins and remove any of the newspaper or tissue paper that might have stuck to it. Mark and cut off the 'V' shapes on the bottom of the uprights with a coping saw.

Ensure that the gate moves freely between the guides in the gatehouse and drill a 1/16in (1mm) hole in the centre of the top. Knot one end of the cord and thread it through the hole in the portcullis, the top of the gatehouse and the loose piece of the battlements. Knot the opposite end of the cord and cut to length.

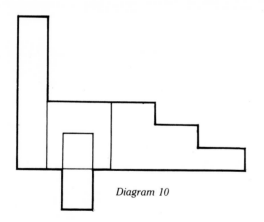
Diagram 10

DIAGRAM 10

Side battlements. Mark and cut out the battlement front-piece (25) and glue to the rear timber walkway (26). Cut the end steps (27) with three equal steps and glue them in position on the walkway. Cut the steps with a tenon saw.

In the centre of the base in the walkway, drill a ⅜in (10mm) hole to a depth of ½in (12mm). Cut the dowel (28) to length and glue in position.

Repeat the whole operation for the second side battlement.

Front battlement. The five pieces of the front battlements (29, 30, 31, 32) are cut out and assembled in the same way as the side battlements. As with the battlements on the towers, cut each battlement section of equal size.

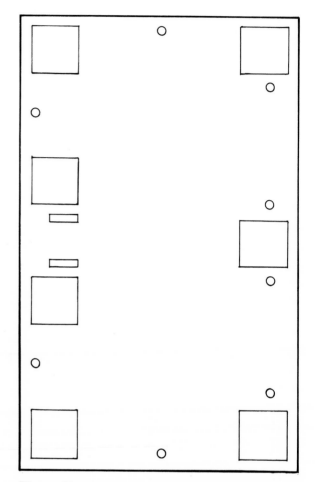
Diagram 11

DIAGRAM 11

When all sections have been constructed, assemble them in position on the base, the towers so as to fit over their respective blocks. Place the rear compartments, the side and front battlements in position, and mark the position of their locating dowels on the base. Drill the holes in the base, the same diameter as the dowels and slot the assemblies into the holes.

Cut the two guide pieces (19a) for the gatehouse and glue them in position on the base.

Portcullis

22. Upright Pieces (5), timber: $3 \times 5/16 \times 5/16$in ($75 \times 9 \times 9$mm)

23. Crosspieces (12), timber: $3/8 \times 5/16 \times 5/16$in ($10 \times 9 \times 9$mm)

24. Top, timber: $3\,5/16 \times 5/16 \times 5/16$in ($85 \times 9 \times 9$mm)
Length of thin cord

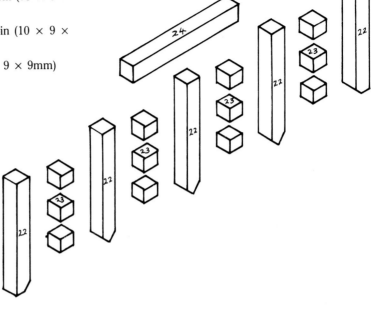

Side Battlements

25. Frontpiece (2), timber: $9 \times 2 \times 3/8$in ($228 \times 50 \times 10$mm)
26. Walkway (2), timber: $9 \times 7/8 \times 7/8$in ($228 \times 22 \times 22$mm)
27. End step (4), timber: $1\,7/8 \times 7/8 \times 7/8$in ($47 \times 22 \times 22$mm)
28. Locating dowels (2): $1 \times 3/8$in diameter (25×10mm diameter)

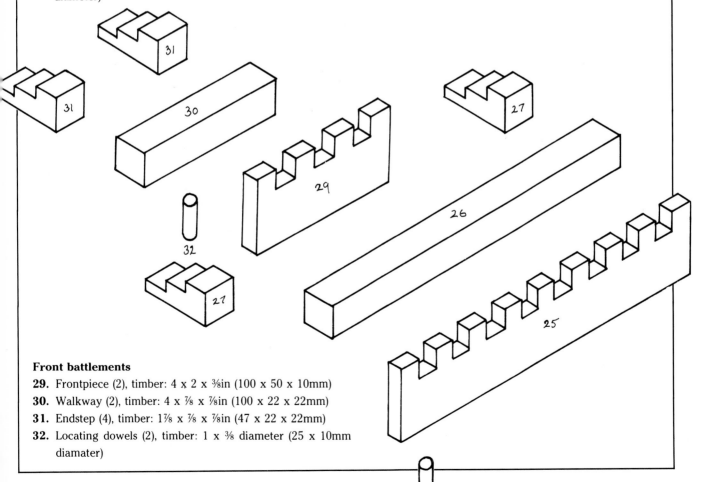

Front battlements

29. Frontpiece (2), timber: $4 \times 2 \times 3/8$in ($100 \times 50 \times 10$mm)
30. Walkway (2), timber: $4 \times 7/8 \times 7/8$in ($100 \times 22 \times 22$mm)
31. Endstep (4), timber: $1\,7/8 \times 7/8 \times 7/8$in ($47 \times 22 \times 22$mm)
32. Locating dowels (2), timber: $1 \times 3/8$ diameter (25×10mm diamater)

DIAGRAM 12

Front ramp. Cut the front and rear plywood pieces (33) to shape. In the front-piece mark and cut out the entrance the same shape and size as the gatehouse. Cut the two ramps (34) and the top (35) and glue the assembly together.

Sand down all the sections and paint. It is advisable to paint the portcullis before installing it in the gatehouse.

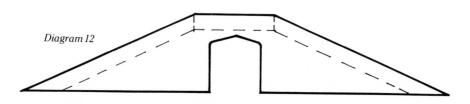

Diagram 12

Front Ramp

33. Front and rear pieces (2), plywood: 23 × 4 × ¼in (584 × 100 × 6mm)
34. Ramps (2), timber: 10 × 2½ × ⅞in (254 × 64 × 22mm)
35. Top, timber: 4¼ × 2½ × ⅞in (107 × 64 × 22mm)

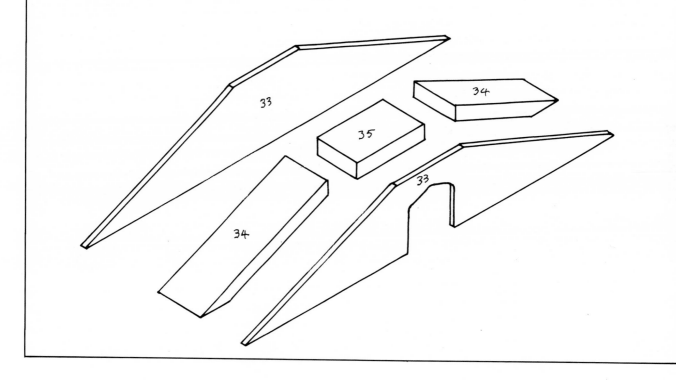

GARAGE

A garage is surely a 'must' for a boy's playroom, and why not a girl's too? This model has two service bays and a roof-top car park.

Busy garage and car park.

DIAGRAM 1 (see page 78)

Garage. On the front wall of the garage (1) mark and cut out the three entrances. The corners should be rounded. Cut these with a coping saw.

DIAGRAM 2

Cut to length the two sides (2 and 3), the rear wall (4) and the inner ramp wall (5), and glue and screw these together. Cut the intermediate wall (6) to length and glue this in position. When doing this, check that the distance between the inner ramp wall and the back wall is equal. Cut the intermediate wall (7) to length and glue this in position. This wall divides the two bays equally. Ensure that the intermediate walls (6 and 7) are flush with the bottom edges of the outer wall.

DIAGRAM 3

Mark a line 1½in (37mm) down from the top of the outside walls and glue ½in (12mm) pieces of timber (8) to each wall to support the plywood roof pieces. Ensure these pieces of timber finish flush with the top of the intermediate walls. Cut the two support pieces (9) for the ramp and glue these in position on the inside of the rear wall and the inner ramp wall. Ensure these two supports finish flush with the other roof supports. Cut out and glue in position on the support pieces the plywood roof and ramp (10 and 11).

DIAGRAM 4

Base. Cut the base (12) to size. Place the garage building in position so that one corner is flush with a corner on the base. On the other three corners, mark a suitable radius and cut to shape with a coping saw. The garage building can be glued permanently in position, or left so as to be detachable.

DIAGRAM 5 (see also Materials, page 81)

Fuel pumps. Mark and cut out the base and the roof pieces (13). Do this by clamping both pieces together, and cutting out with a tenon saw. This will ensure both pieces are identical. Cut the three pieces of timber for the petrol pumps (14) and glue these in position on the plywood base. Cut the two pieces of timber for the support pillars (15) and glue these in position on the base. Glue the roof section in position on the top of the two pillars directly above the base.

When assembled, the petrol pumps, like the main garage building, can be permanently glued in position or left free standing. If glued in position on the base they should be placed halfway between the front of the garage and the front of the base. This will allow your toy motor cars to pass on both sides of the petrol pumps as in real garages.

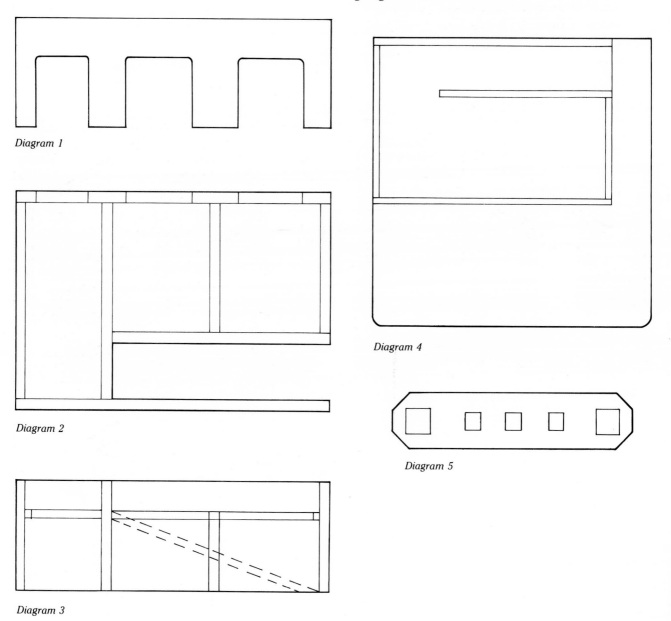

Diagram 1

Diagram 2

Diagram 3

Diagram 4

Diagram 5

MATERIALS FOR GARAGE (see also pages 80, 81)

1. Front, timber: $18 \times 6 \times \frac{5}{8}$in ($460 \times 150 \times 15$mm)
2. Side, timber: $10\frac{3}{4} \times 6 \times \frac{5}{8}$in ($275 \times 150 \times 15$mm)
3. Side, timber: $6\frac{7}{8} \times 6 \times \frac{5}{8}$in ($175 \times 150 \times 15$mm)
4. Rear wall, timber: $18 \times 6 \times \frac{3}{8}$in ($460 \times 150 \times 15$mm)
5. Inner, timber: $12\frac{3}{4} \times 6 \times \frac{5}{8}$in ($325 \times 150 \times 15$mm)

Ramp wall

6. Intermediate wall, timber: $10\frac{3}{4} \times 4\frac{3}{8} \times \frac{5}{8}$in ($275 \times 112 \times 15$mm)
7. Intermediate wall, timber: $6\frac{7}{8} \times 4\frac{3}{8} \times \frac{5}{8}$in ($175 \times 112 \times 15$mm)
8. Supports (4), timber: $5\frac{3}{4} \times \frac{5}{8} \times \frac{5}{8}$in ($145 \times 15 \times 15$mm)
   Supports (1), timber: $6\frac{7}{8} \times \frac{5}{8} \times \frac{5}{8}$in ($175 \times 15 \times 15$mm)
   Supports (1), timber: $5\frac{1}{2} \times \frac{5}{8} \times \frac{5}{8}$in ($140 \times 15 \times 15$mm)
   Supports (1), timber: $3\frac{1}{4} \times \frac{5}{8} \times \frac{5}{8}$in ($82 \times 15 \times 15$mm)
9. Ramp support (2), timber: $12\frac{1}{2} \times \frac{5}{8} \times \frac{5}{8}$in ($320 \times 15 \times 15$mm)

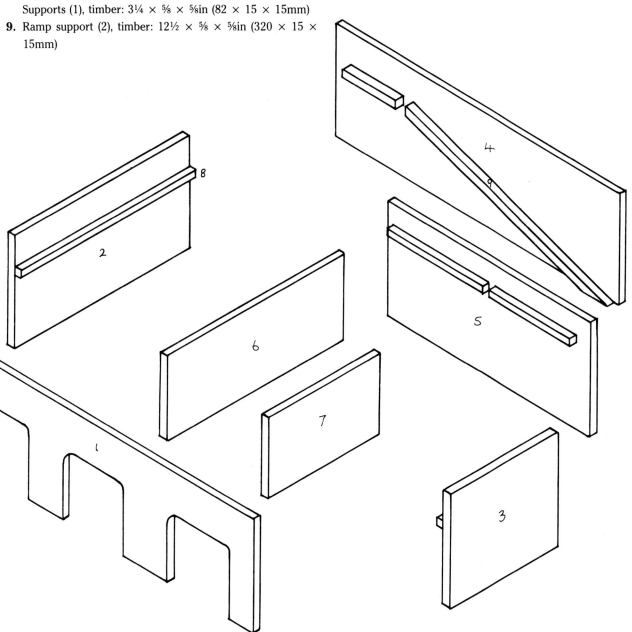

Base & roof

10. Roof, plywood: 16¾ × 10¾ × ¼in (425 × 275 × 6mm)
11. Ramp, plywood: 13¾ × 3¼ × ¼in (349 × 82 × 6mm)
12. Base, plywood: 21 × 21 × ¼in (535 × 535 × 6mm)

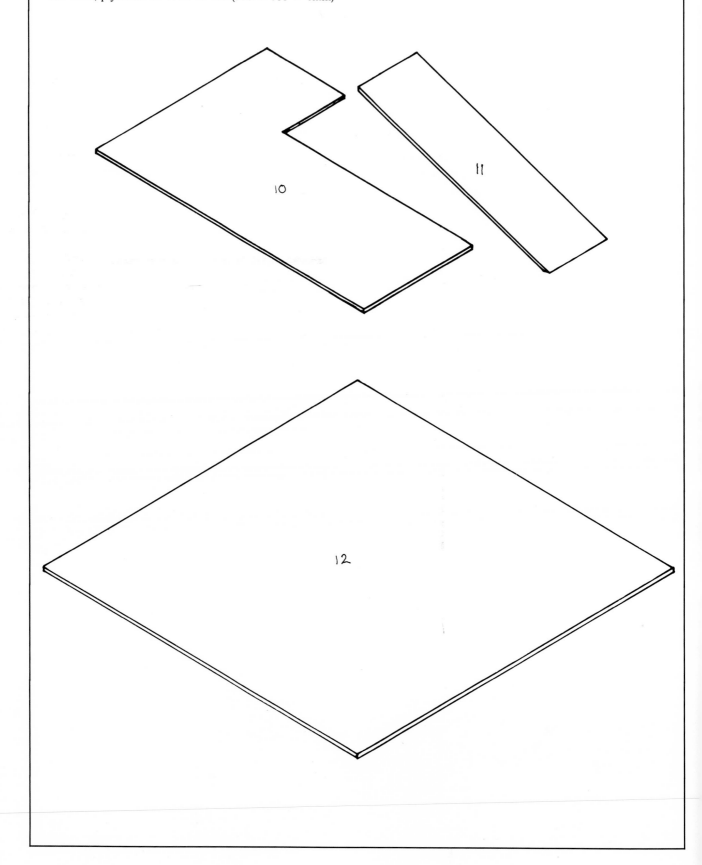

Fuel pumps

13. Base and roof (2), plywood: 9 × 2 × ¼in (230 × 50 × 6mm)
14. Fuel pump (2), timber: 1½ × ¾ × ⅝in (37 × 18 × 15mm)
15. Pillars (2), timber: 3 × ⅞ × ⅞in (75 × 22 × 22mm)

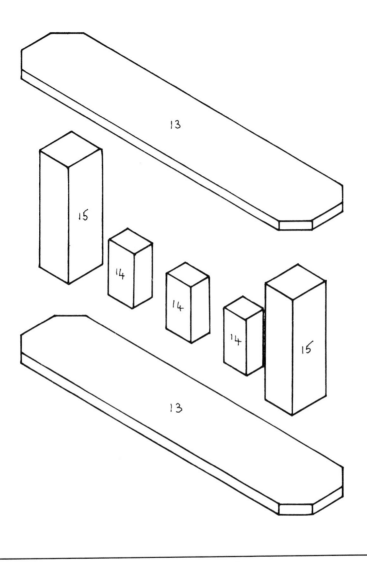

COOKER/STOVE

Most children like to imitate their parents, and a miniature cooker will enable them to do this without hindrance to the parents, or damage to the child! The toy is made with substantial plywood and timber so that it will stand firmly on the floor.

DIAGRAM 1 (see also page 85)

All the joints are simply built. To complete the model, two lengths of piano hinge and two small catches will be required for the opening doors.

Main frame. Glue and screw together the two sides (1), the base (2), the shelf (3) and the two front rails (4). Ensure the rails are the correct distance apart for the door, and that the whole assembly is square.

On the back panel (5) round off the two top corners with a coping saw to the required radius, 1¼in (30mm). Glue and screw the panel in position.

DIAGRAM 2

Screw one side of a hinge in position on the door (6 and 7). Attach the door to the main frame of the cooker by screwing the opposite side of the hinge in position on the front rails. When doing this, ensure that the edge of the door is square with the main frame. This will allow the door to fit flush with the main frame when closed. Cut both door handles (8) to shape with a coping saw and glue in position.

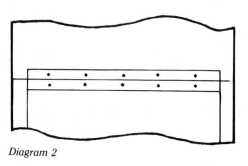

Diagram 2

DIAGRAM 3

Top section and control panel. Glue the top section (9) in position on the main frame. Glue the two pieces of the control panel (10 and 11) together. Check that the back piece extends ⅞in (22mm) below the front panel and that it fits under the top section. When this is done, glue the two pieces to the main frame work.

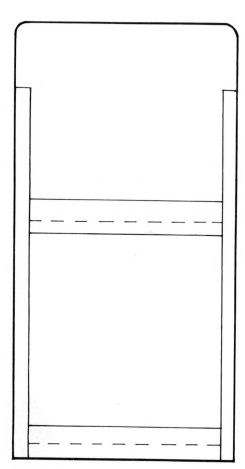

Diagram 1

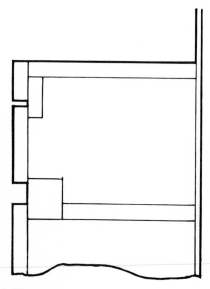

Diagram 3

What's cooking?

DIAGRAM 4

Cut the three pieces of timber (12, 13) and glue them in position around the edge of the top section. For a neater appearance, cut mitre joints on the corners. Cut the remaining three pieces of timber (14, 15) to length and glue in position to form four equal squares. With the hole saw, cut out four circles (16) to represent the rings, and glue these in position in the centre of each square.

Also with the hole saw, cut out four circles of plywood (17) for the coloured knobs and glue these in position on the control panel.

The rings and control panel knobs will all have a ⅜in (9mm) hole in the centre from the hole saw. These can either be left, or filled before painting.

The catches should now be fitted to both doors. There are many different types of catch, and each will have its own fixing instructions, which should be followed.

Sand down the whole assembly and paint to the colours of your choice.

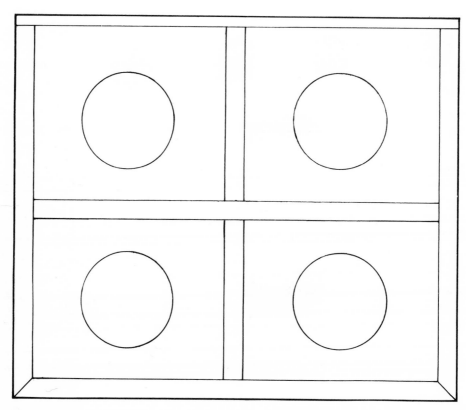

Diagram 4

MATERIALS FOR COOKER/STOVE

Main frame

1. Sides (2), chipboard or plywood: 19½ × 9 × ¾in (495 × 230 × 18mm)
2. Base, chipboard or plywood: 10½ × 7¼ × ¾in (265 × 184 × 18mm)
3. Shelf, chipboard or plywood: 10½ × 7¼ × ¾in (265 × 184 × 18mm)
4. Front rail (2): 10½ × 1⅞ × 1⅞in (265 × 47 × 47mm)
5. Back panel, plywood: 23 × 12 × ¼in (585 × 305 × 6mm)
6. Door top, chipboard or plywood: 12 × 3¾ × ¾in (305 × 96 × 18mm)
7. Door bottom, chipboard or plywood: 12 × 11¼ × ¾in (305 × 285 × 18mm)
8. Door handles (2), timber: 2 × 1 × ⅝in (50 × 25 × 15mm)
9. Top section, plywood and chipboard: 12 × 9 × ¾in (305 × 230 × 18mm)
10. Control panel backpiece, timber: 10½ × 2 × ¾in (265 × 50 × 18mm)
11. Control panel frontpiece, chipboard or plywood: 12 × 2 × ¾in (305 × 50 × 18mm)
12. Surrounds (1), timber: 12 × ½ × ½in (305 × 12 × 12mm)
13. Surrounds (2), timber: 9¾ × ½ × ½in (248 × 12 × 12mm)
14. Surrounds (1), timber: 11 × ½ × ½in (280 × 12 × 12mm)
15. Surrounds (2), timber: 4½ × ½ × ½in (112 × 12 × 12mm)
16. Rings (4), timber: 2⅜ diameter × ⅝in (60 × 15mm)
17. Control knobs (4): 1¼ diameter × ¼in (30 × 6mm) plywood

    Plastic doorcatches (2)

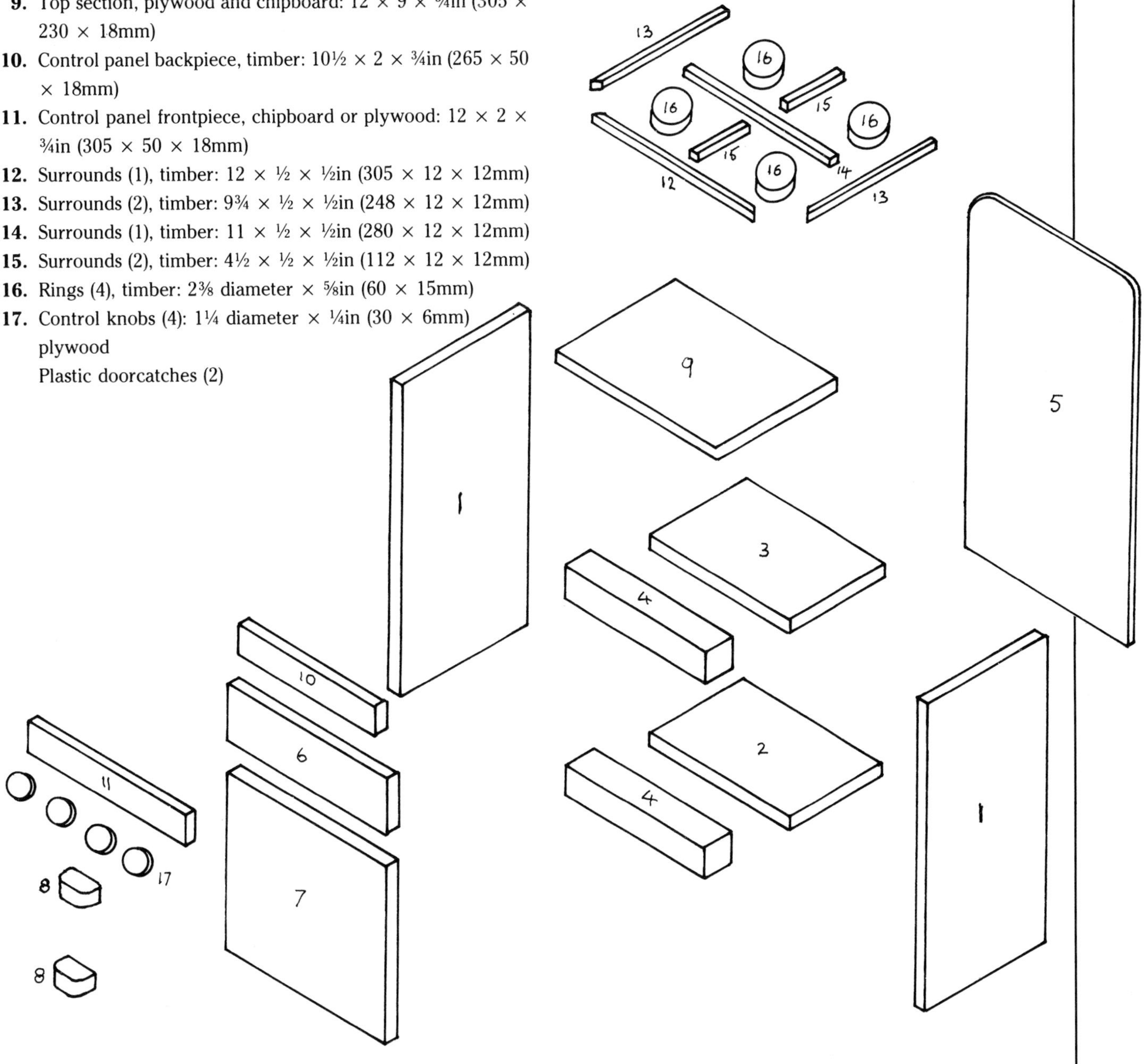

WASHING MACHINE

This washing machine makes an excellent companion for the cooker and, if doubled up as a tumble-drier, will complete the toy kitchen equipment. The washing machine has a hand-operated revolving drum, but this is constructed in such a way that children cannot harm themselves. As for the cooker, a length of piano hinge and catch will be required for the door.

DIAGRAM 1 (see also page 89)

Main frame. Glue and screw the two sides (1) the base (2) and the top (3) together, ensuring the frame is square.

DIAGRAM 2

On the front panel (4) mark out the two openings, leaving a central bar and 2in (50mm) diameter central circle.

To cut out each section, first drill a 1in (25mm) diameter hole in each corner, next to the central bar, with a twist bit. When doing this, place a scrap piece of timber under the twist bit to prevent the plywood from splitting. With a coping saw, remove the remainder. To do this, remove the blade from the saw frame and place it through one of the holes. Re-connect the blade in the frame and cut around the section. Remove the saw from this section and repeat the operation in the other section.

DIAGRAM 3

Make the support piece (5) for the drum by marking out a 2in (50mm) diameter circle on a piece of timber. Drill out a 1in (25mm) hole with a twist bit in the centre of the cir-

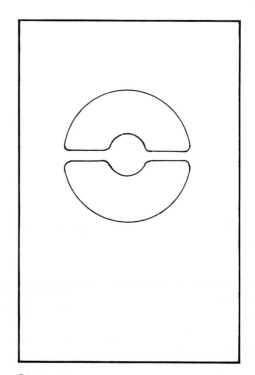

Diagram 2

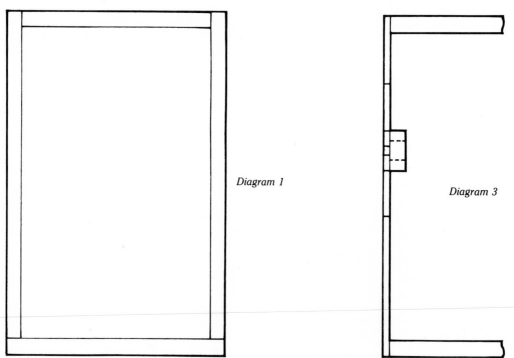

Diagram 1

Diagram 3

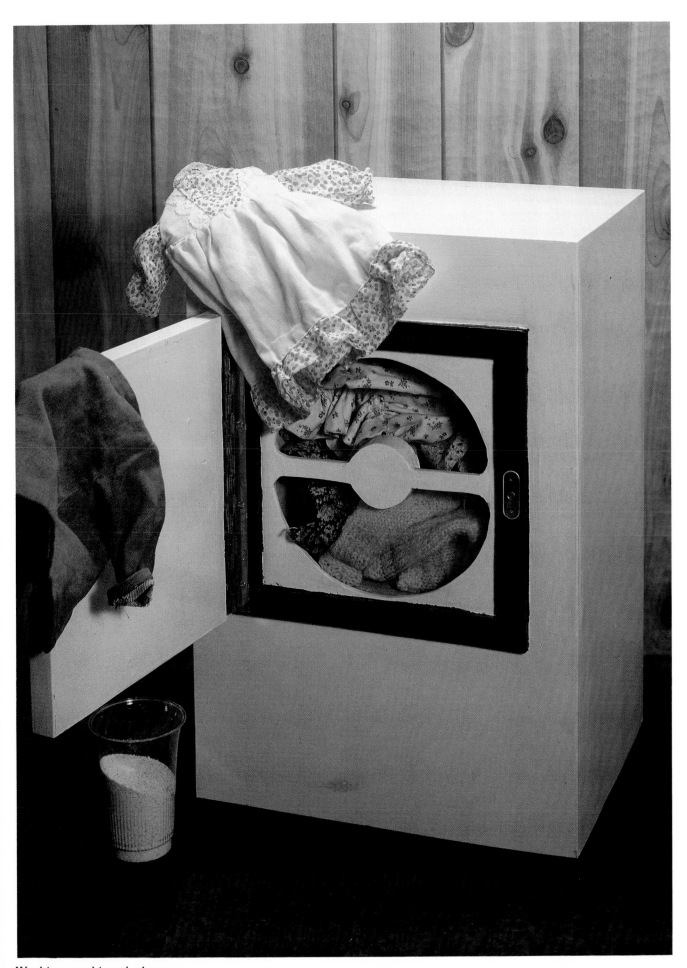

Washing machine. A clean toy.

cle and, with a coping saw, cut out the 2in (50mm) circle.

Glue the support piece in the centre of the cut out section on the front panel and glue and screw the front panel in position on the main frame.

DIAGRAM 4

Revolving drum. In the centre of the base (6) mark and drill out a 1in (25mm) diameter hole. Ensure the hole is drilled vertically. Glue and screw the four sides of the drum (7 and 8) to the base.

Cut the central pivot dowel (9) to length and insert it in the hole in the base and glue in position. The end of the dowel, opposite to the base, should be flush with the top of the drum and an equal distance from each side.

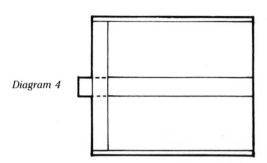

Diagram 4

Place the main frame of the washing machine face down on your working surface and fit the revolving drum in position, locating the central pivot dowel in the support piece on the front panel.

On the back panel (10) mark out a 1in (25mm) hole for the pivot dowel to pass through in exactly the same position as the central circle on the front panel.

Place the back panel in position, with the pivot dowel protruding through the hole. Before screwing the back panel into position permanently, check that the drum revolves freely. If it does not, then remove the back panel and the drum, and sand down both ends of the central pivot dowel until it does.

DIAGRAM 5

Turning disc handle. Mark and cut out the turning disc (11). In the centre of the disc and ¾in (18mm) from the edge, drill two ⅛in (3mm) holes. Glue and screw via the hole on the edge of the disc, the turning handle (12). Via the hole in the centre, glue and screw the disc to the end of the central pivot dowel. Allow the glue to dry and again check that the drum revolves freely.

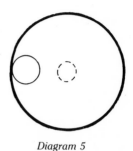

Diagram 5

DIAGRAM 6

Door. Glue the four pieces of the door surround (13, 14) in position on the front panel to form a square.

On one edge of the door (15) cut a rebate to the depth of the piano hinge and screw the hinge onto the door. Cut a recess on the opposite edge of the door to house the magnetic catch.

Screw the door to the surround and fix the second part of the magnetic catch in place on the surround. Ensure that the door is square with the surround.

Sand down the whole assembly and paint, taking care not to allow any paint to prevent the drum and handle from revolving.

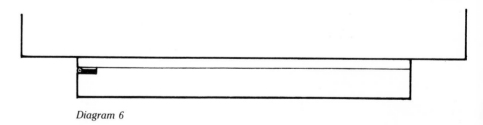

Diagram 6

MATERIALS FOR WASHING MACHINE

Main frame

1. Sides (2), plywood: 17¼ × 9 × ¾in (438 × 228 × 18mm)
2. Base, plywood: 10½ × 9 × ¾in (268 × 228 × 18mm)
3. Top, plywood: 12 × 9 × ¾in (305 × 228 × 18mm)
4. Front panel, plywood: 18 × 12 × ¼in (458 × 305 × 6mm)
5. Support piece, timber: ⅞ × 2in diameter (22 × 50mm)

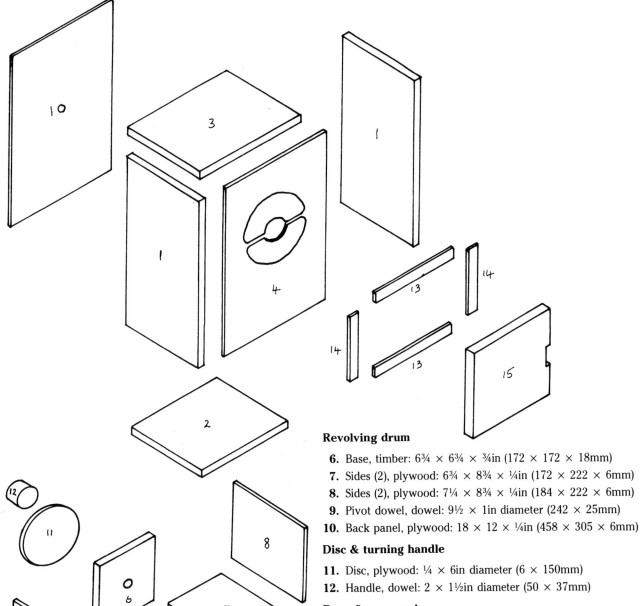

Revolving drum

6. Base, timber: 6¾ × 6¾ × ¾in (172 × 172 × 18mm)
7. Sides (2), plywood: 6¾ × 8¾ × ¼in (172 × 222 × 6mm)
8. Sides (2), plywood: 7¼ × 8¾ × ¼in (184 × 222 × 6mm)
9. Pivot dowel, dowel: 9½ × 1in diameter (242 × 25mm)
10. Back panel, plywood: 18 × 12 × ¼in (458 × 305 × 6mm)

Disc & turning handle

11. Disc, plywood: ¼ × 6in diameter (6 × 150mm)
12. Handle, dowel: 2 × 1½in diameter (50 × 37mm)

Door & surrounds

13. Surround (2), plywood: 9 × 1 × ¼in (228 × 25 × 6mm)
14. Surround (2), plywood: 7 × 1 × ¼in (178 × 25 × 6mm)
15. Door, plywood: 9 × 9 × ¾in (228 × 228 × 18mm)
    Piano hinge: 9in (228mm)
    Magnetic catch

5
GARDEN TOYS

WIGWAM

I wonder if Cowboys and Indians is still as popular with children as it used to be? Even if it is not, children will surely enjoy this wigwam, or tepee, which will provide them with an ideal atmosphere for their games.

The wigwam consists of two pairs of sides, bolted together. One pair of sides has the top open to allow some light into the interior, and one of these sides has the entrance cut in it. When dismantled, the four sides can be stacked flat or stored away.

DIAGRAM 1

All the timber used for the outside edges of the framework is bevelled to an angle of 75 degrees. This allows the sides to fit together flush when assembled.

If possible, get your timber merchant to cut the angle on the timber. This will save a great deal of time and make assembly easier. If you cannot do this, then plane each side piece to the correct angle with a jack plane.

DIAGRAM 2

Closed panels. Mark and cut the triangular hardboard panels (1). To do this, mark the centre of the panel on one edge. From this mark draw lines to the two opposite corners to form a triangle. Cut the side and bottom pieces (2, 3) to length. Cut the angles on each end. Glue and screw into position flush with the edges of the panel (see diagram 2 below). Cut the intermediate pieces (4, 5). Glue and screw in position.

Repeat the operation for the second closed panel. Where the two panels meet at the top, cut the framework on both panels to an angle of 45 degrees. When all four panels are assembled, this will allow some clearance to manoeuvre the panels into position.

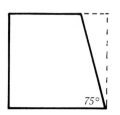

Diagram 1

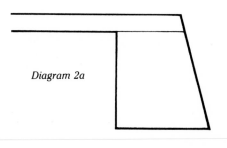

Diagram 2a

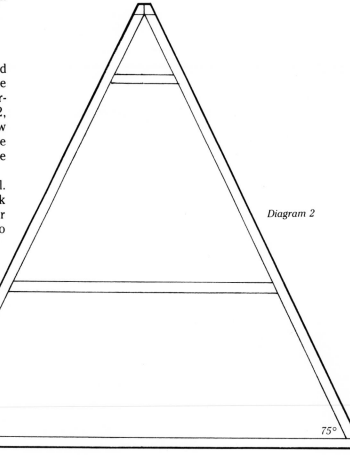

Diagram 2

Injun country.

DIAGRAM 3 (see over)

Open top panels. Cut out the triangular hardboard panels (6) as for the other sides but with these panels, measure 9in (225mm) down each side from the top. Mark lines at 30 degrees across from each side and cut out.

On the inside face of the hardboard panel (6), mark lines 1in (25mm) in from the two outside edges.Cut the pieces of timber for the edges and the bottom (7, 8). The angles on the ends are the same as for the closed panels. Glue and screw these in position, with the bevelled edges in the same position as the closed panels, but set 1in (25mm) from the edge (see diagram 3A overleaf). Cut and glue the intermediate pieces (9, 10) of the framework in position.

Repeat this for the second side. Before glueing the framework to the hardboard panel on the second side, mark and cut out the opening. Do this in two stages. Firstly, with a panel saw, cut along each side to a depth of 7½in (187mm). Then, with a coping saw, remove the bottom section and cut out the remaining semi-circular section.

When all the sides are completed, assemble and check that they fit together with the side edges flush and that the assembly sits flat on the floor and does not rock. When this is achieved, mark and drill the holes for the bolts. Drill four holes, two on each edge, ¼in (6mm) in diameter, 9in (225mm) from the bottom and 15in (375mm) from the point on the closed side.

Ensure the drill bit penetrates the framework of both sides. Insert the bolts from the outside and screw the nut on from the inside. The assembly will be very rigid when all the bolts are inserted and the nuts tightened up.

Sand down and paint each side separately. If desired, you can paint various Red Indian symbols.

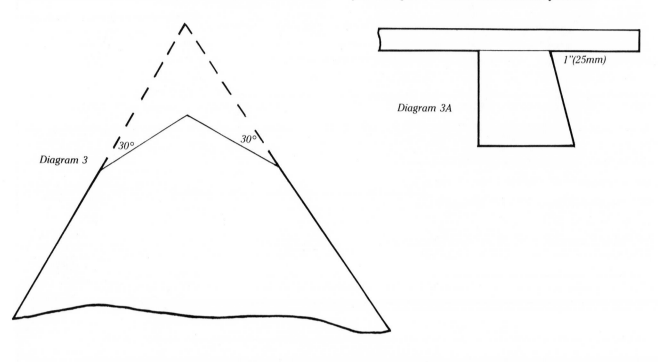

Diagram 3

Diagram 3A

1"(25mm)

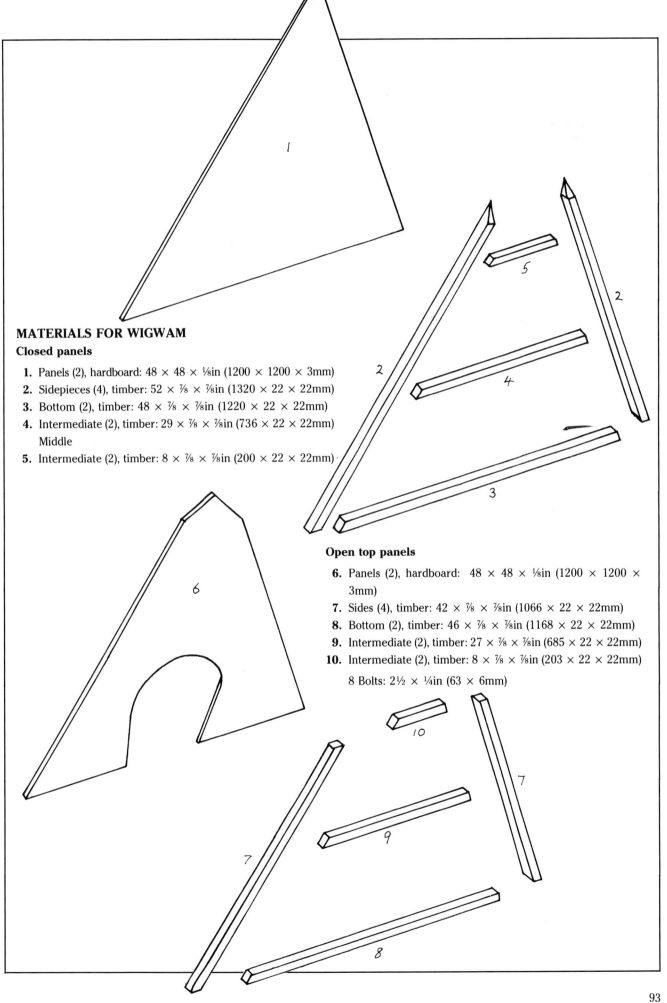

MATERIALS FOR WIGWAM
Closed panels

1. Panels (2), hardboard: 48 × 48 × ⅛in (1200 × 1200 × 3mm)
2. Sidepieces (4), timber: 52 × ⅞ × ⅞in (1320 × 22 × 22mm)
3. Bottom (2), timber: 48 × ⅞ × ⅞in (1220 × 22 × 22mm)
4. Intermediate (2), timber: 29 × ⅞ × ⅞in (736 × 22 × 22mm)
   Middle
5. Intermediate (2), timber: 8 × ⅞ × ⅞in (200 × 22 × 22mm)

Open top panels

6. Panels (2), hardboard: 48 × 48 × ⅛in (1200 × 1200 × 3mm)
7. Sides (4), timber: 42 × ⅞ × ⅞in (1066 × 22 × 22mm)
8. Bottom (2), timber: 46 × ⅞ × ⅞in (1168 × 22 × 22mm)
9. Intermediate (2), timber: 27 × ⅞ × ⅞in (685 × 22 × 22mm)
10. Intermediate (2), timber: 8 × ⅞ × ⅞in (203 × 22 × 22mm)

    8 Bolts: 2½ × ¼in (63 × 6mm)

WASHING LINE AND PROP

This toy is easily made using the basic tools and, on hot summer days, will give children lots of pleasure in the garden or backyard, as they hang out the family washing.

Junior clothes-line with props.

DIAGRAM 1

Clothes posts. On the base (1) mark the centre by drawing diagonal lines from corner to corner. Around the centre of the base, mark a 1in (25mm) square and cut out the square. Cut the square by removing the bulk of the wood with a 1in (25mm) diameter twist bit and remove the remaining corner pieces with a ½in (12mm) chisel.

DIAGRAM 2

On the end of the post (2) mark out a 1in (25mm) square and also a line around the post to a depth of the thickness of the plywood base. With a tenon saw, cut around this square to the depth of the thickness of the base.

On the line around the post, cut away the sections of timber, leaving the 1in (25mm) square. The post can then

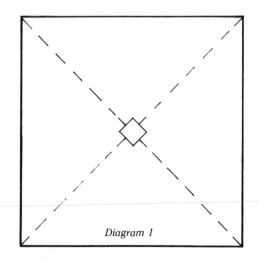

Diagram 1

94

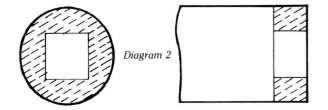

Diagram 2

DIAGRAM 4

Clothes prop. Make the clothes prop (4) from a 1in (25mm) square piece of timber. In one end of the prop cut a 1in (25mm) deep 'v' shape. This will enable the prop to support the washing line strung between the two posts.

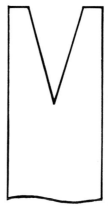

Diagram 4

be fitted in the hole in the base. Check that the square on the end of the post will fit into the square hole cut in the base. When this is achieved, put the base to one side.

DIAGRAM 3

Take the post and 3in (75mm) from the opposite end to the square, drill a ½in (12mm) diameter hole in the centre of the post. Turn the post through 90 degrees, and 3¾in (94mm) from the same end, drill a second ½in (12mm) diameter hole.

Cut the crosspiece (3) from ½in (12mm) diameter dowel and insert these into the two holes. If any difficulty is found fitting the crosspieces into the holes then, with sandpaper, round off the ends of the crosspieces, and this will enable them to fit into the holes more easily.

When the crosspieces are inserted, check that an equal length protrudes at each side of the post, and when centralized, glue in position.

Take the base, apply some glue to the inside of the hole cut in the centre, and then fit the square end of the post into the base and allow it to dry. Check that the post is vertical.

The whole operation should be repeated for the second clothes post.

When both posts and prop are completed, rub down with fine grade sandpaper and paint to the colours of your choice.

For the model I made, I chose bright blue for the posts and prop, and used a bright yellow washing line, which gives a pleasant contrast of colour.

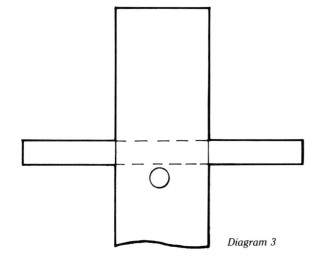

Diagram 3

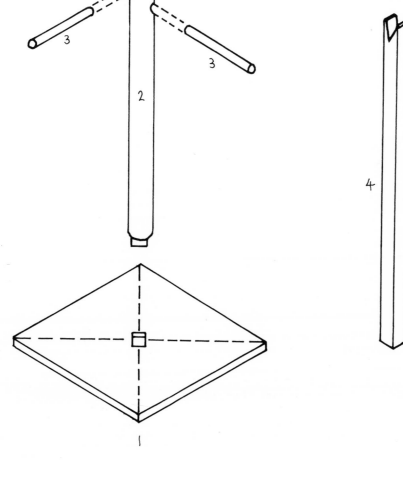

MATERIALS FOR WASHING LINE AND PROP
Clothes posts

1. Base (2), plywood: 12 × 12 × ¾in (305 × 305 × 18mm)
2. Posts (2), dowel: 30 × 2in diameter (762 × 50mm)
3. Crosspieces (4), dowel: 6 × ½in diameter (150 × 12mm)

Prop

4. Prop (1), timber: 30 × 1 × 1in (762 × 25 × 25mm)

WHEELBARROW

In the garden, a wheelbarrow is essential, and children will find no end of uses for it. They can help carry plants, soil, sand, not to mention dolls and toys, and with this sturdy design, they can even carry one another about!

DIAGRAM 1 (see Materials, page 100)

Mark and cut out the two sides (1). To ensure the two sides are identical, clamp them both together with a G clamp (US. 'C' clamp) and cut both together.

When both sides are cut, shape each handle with a spokeshave for an easier grip.

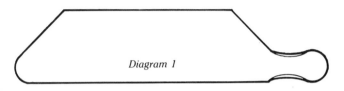

Diagram 1

DIAGRAM 2

Mark out the base of the wheelbarrow (2). Do this by marking a line in the centre of the base along the longest length. At one end, mark 6in (150mm) on each side of the lines and at the other end mark 3in (75mm) each side of the line. Allow for the thickness of the sides, ⅞in (22mm) and join the marks together and cut out the shape with a tenon saw.

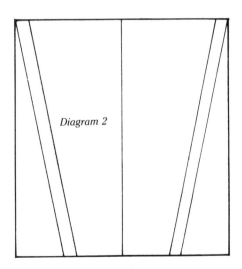

Diagram 2

DIAGRAM 3

When the base is cut out and the angles determined, place the front piece (3) and the rear piece (4) in position on the base and mark out the angles on the bottom of both pieces. Square the lines, round and cut to shape.

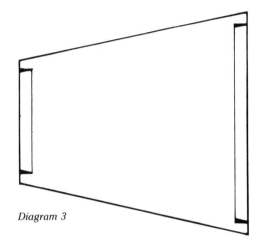

Diagram 3

DIAGRAM 4

Mark out the curve on the top of each piece and cut to shape with a coping saw. Glue and screw the two sides and the front and rear pieces to the base and to each other. Check that they are vertical to the base.

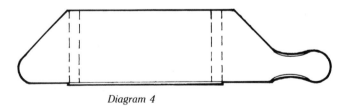

Diagram 4

DIAGRAM 5 (see over)

Mark and drill out a hole at the end of each side for the axle. Using a sliding bevel, set this to the angle of the base and move it 3½in (87mm) along the side piece towards the front. Mark a line across the two side pieces.

Alternatively, mark 3½in (87mm) along each piece from the end of the base and joint these two marks together. From these marks, square a line along the outside of the side piece and 1in (25mm) from the bottom mark the centre of the axle. With a twist bit, drill a ⅞in (22mm) hole keeping the bit at the correct angle. With the first side place a scrap piece of timber behind the hole and

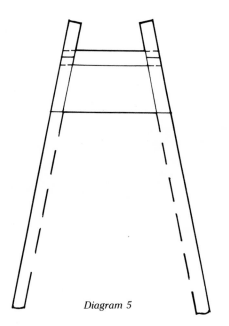

Diagram 5

DIAGRAM 7

Cut the two legs (8) to length and mark the angle required for the leg to fit into the corner of the side and rear pieces. Shape the legs either by planing or sawing to the required angle.

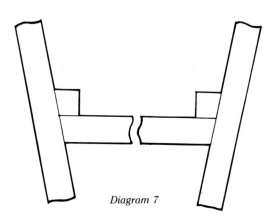

Diagram 7

allow the bit to enter the scrap piece, so as not to splinter the inside face of the timber. Remove the scrap piece of timber when the hole is drilled. Drill through the second side until the point of the bit shows through the timber. Take out the bit, place the bit through the hole already drilled in the first side and complete drilling the second piece.

Sand down the assembly and paint. It is advisable to paint the wheel before fixing. As the toy will be used outside, follow the instructions on painting for exterior use.

DIAGRAM 6

Cut out the wheel (5) with a coping saw and drill a 1in (25mm) hole in the centre. In the axle (6) drill two ¼in (6mm) holes equal distance from each end and 1¼in (30mm) apart.

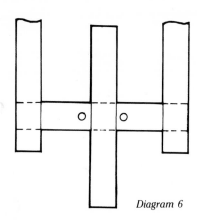

Diagram 6

Push the axle through the hole in one side and locate the wheel on the axle. Continue to push the axle through to the hole in the second side. Glue the axle in position. With a smoothing plane remove the ends of the axle and leave them flush with the sides. Insert the two dowels (7) in the holes drilled in the axle, to centralise the wheel.

Wheelbarrow and produce. Off to market?

MATERIALS FOR WHEELBARROW

1. Sides (2), timber: 30 × 6½ × ⅞in (760 × 165 × 22mm)
2. Base, plywood: 14 × 14½ × ¼in (355 × 365 × 6mm)
3. Front, timber: 6 × 6½ × ⅞in (150 × 165 × 22mm)
4. Rear, timber: 12 × 6½ × ⅞in (305 × 165 × 22mm)
5. Wheel, timber: 5½ diameter × ⅞in (140 × 22mm)
6. Axle, dowel: 5½ × ⅞in diameter (140 × 22mm)
7. Dowels (2), dowel: 2 × ¼in diameter (50 × 6mm)
8. Legs (2), timber: 12 × ⅞ × ⅞in (305 × 22 × 22mm)

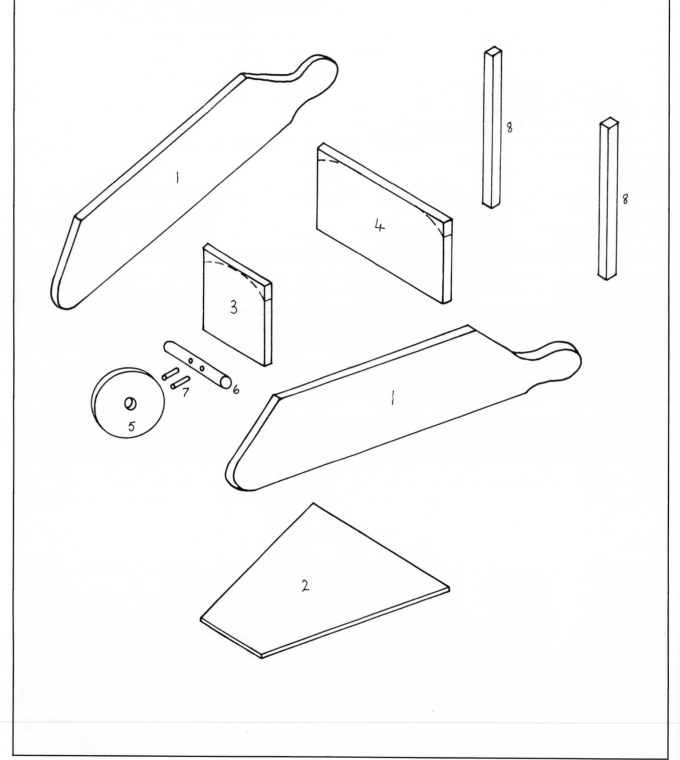

TABLE AND BENCHES

A small version of a kitchen table and benches is always popular with children. In summer they can form a centrepiece for picnics, and in cooler weather the table and benches can be even more useful in a playroom.

To make the table top, a pair of sash (or bar) clamps (see Tools Section, pages 9-10) would be an advantage, and you will also need a mortice marking gauge for the accurate marking out of the mortice and tenon joints in the bases.

Table top. Make the table top from the two pieces of timber (1). Joint these together using the dowel method, glue and clamp together. If you have difficulty in obtaining wood 12in (300mm) wide, then by using the dowel method, you can join four 6in (150mm) pieces together to obtain the same size of table top.

DIAGRAM 1

Base. Make the base from the two legs (2), the two top supports (3) the bottom support (4) and the bottom rail (5).

With the mortice marking gauge, on the top of one leg, mark a tenon one-third the width of the wood, and to the depth of the top support 2in (50mm). Cut out the tenon and reduce its length to 8in (200mm) so that it has four shoulders.

DIAGRAM 2

In the centre of the leg 4in (100mm) from the bottom, mark out a mortice hole for the bottom rail and cut out. Remove the wood from the mortice by using a twist bit, and the remainder with a chisel.

Decide on what shape the legs are to be cut. You can make this shape as simple or as intricate as you wish. You can even leave them with straight edges. When you have decided what shape, if any, you require, mark and cut this shape out with a coping saw. Mark, drill and countersink two ¼in (6mm) holes, 2in (50mm) from each side and 1in (25mm) from the bottom. These holes are for the screws which will secure the bottom support to the legs.

Repeat this whole operation for the second leg.

DIAGRAM 3

On the two top supports (3) mark the mortice holes and cut these out. Check that the tenons on the legs will fit into these mortice holes. On the ends of each top support, mark a semi-circle and cut this shape out. Also, 2in (50mm) from each end and in the centre, drill ¼in (6mm) holes and countersink them. The legs will be screwed to the table top through these holes.

DIAGRAM 4 (see page 104)

On the bottom two supports (4) at 6in (150mm) in from each end, square the lines around the supports and, with

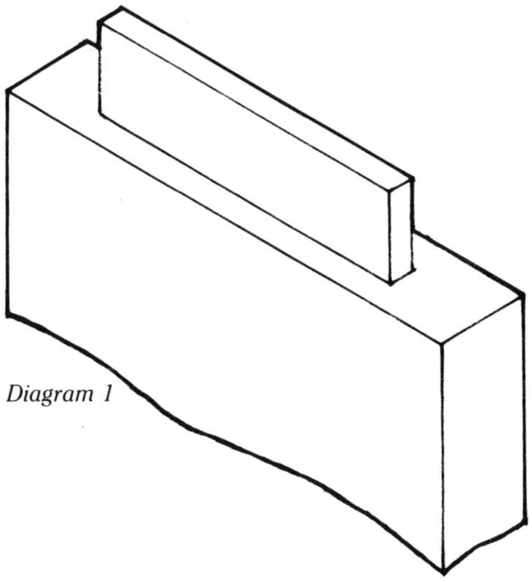

Diagram 1

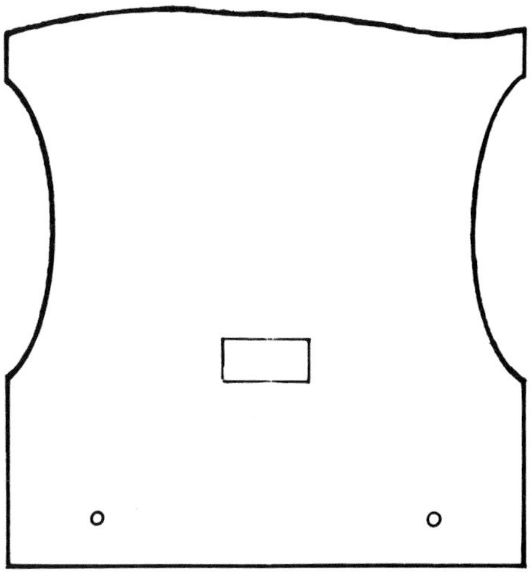

Diagram 2

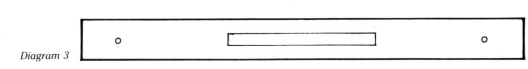

Diagram 3

MATERIALS FOR TABLE AND BENCHES

Table Top

1. Table Top (2), timber: 36 × 12 × 2in (914 × 305 × 50mm)
(4), timber: 36 × 6 × 2in (914 × 150 × 50mm)

Base

2. Legs (2), timber: 18 × 12 × 2in (457 × 305 × 50mm)
(4), timber: 18 × 6 × 2in (457 × 150 × 50mm)

3. Top supports (2), timber: 24 × 2 × 2in (609 × 50 × 50mm)

4. Bottom supports (2), timber: 24 × 2 × 2in (609 × 50 × 50mm)

5. Bottom rail (1), timber: 32 × 2 × 2in (812 × 50 × 50mm)

6. Wedges (2), timber: 1½ × 1½ × ½in (37 × 37 × 12mm)

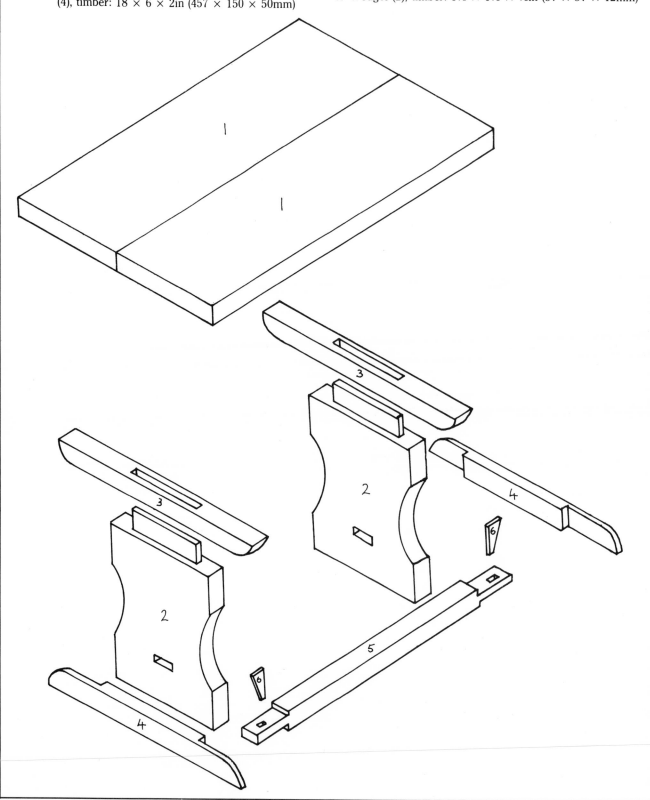

Benches

7. Top (2), timber: 36 × 12 × 2in (914 × 305 × 50mm)
   or (4), timber: 36 × 6 × 2in (914 × 150 × 50mm)
8. Legs (4), timber: 12 × 12 × 2in (305 × 305 × 50mm)
   or (8), timber: 12 × 6 × 2 (305 × 150 × 50mm)
9. Rails (2), timber: 34 × 2 × 2in (863 × 50 × 50mm)
10. Wedges (4), timber: 1½ × 1½ × ½in (37 × 37 × 12mm)

Screws Gauge 8

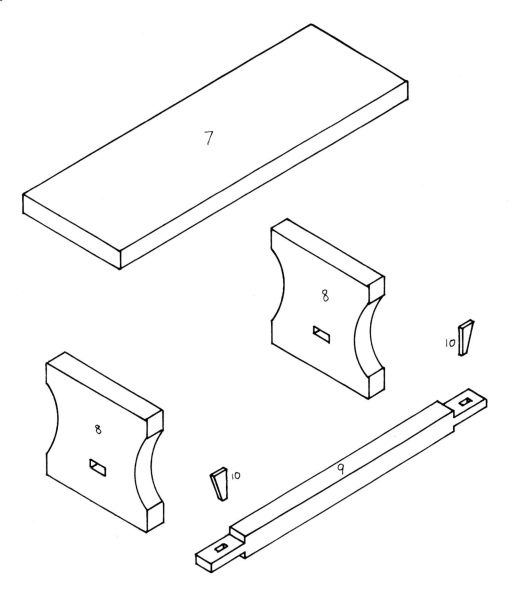

the marking gauge, gauge a line, half the width of the support, around the end.

With a tenon saw, cut these sections out. Mark a semicircle on the end of each support to match the top supports, and cut these out.

DIAGRAM 5

On the bottom rail (5) with the marking gauge, mark a 1in (25mm) tenon, 4in (100mm) from each end. Cut these out with a tenon saw. Check that these tenons will fit into the mortice holes in each leg. When the tenon on the bottom rail is in place, mark the thickness of the leg on the tenon. Withdraw the bottom rail, and on the tenons, at each end, mark a mortice hole ½in (12mm) wide and 1in (25mm) long. Extend the mortice hole ¼in (6mm) beyond the line you have drawn around the tenon and cut out. This will enable the joint to be pulled up tight when the wedges are inserted.

DIAGRAM 6

The wedges should now be cut out. These should taper from 1½in (38mm) to ½in (12mm). The base can now be assembled. Glue and wedge the top supports to the legs. Using two 3in (75mm) gauge 8 screws, screw the bottom support to the legs, ensuring that the two pieces of wood are flush with each other.

Apply glue to the tenons on each end of the bottom rail and insert these into the mortice holes in the legs. Apply some glue to the back of each wedge and insert these into the mortice hole cut in each tenon. Gently tap each wedge home until the joint is pulled up tight. Check that the assembly is square.

Using four 3in (75mm) gauge 8 screws, screw the table top to the base assembly via the holes already drilled in the top rails.

Benches. The benches are made in the same way as the table top, but the base assemblies have no top or bottom supports, and the rails are 2in (50mm) longer than the bottom rail for the table. This is done to give more stability to the bench.

If you have shaped the legs of the table, then shape the legs of each bench to match. The bench top is secured to the base assembly by glueing and screwing through the top into each leg with four 3in (75mm) gauge 8 screws.

Sand down the table and both benches and apply three coats of exterior quality varnish.

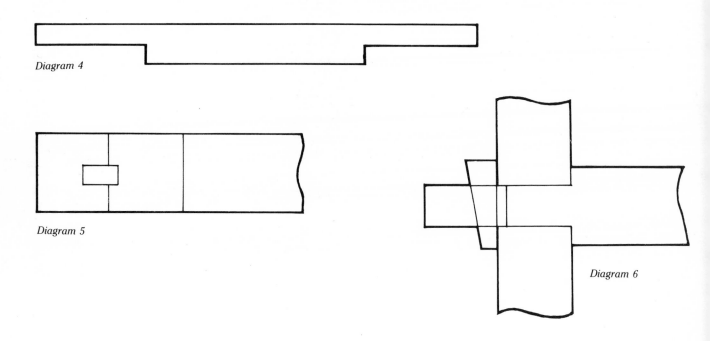

Diagram 4

Diagram 5

Diagram 6

Do you ever pine to make your own garden table and benches?

Index

OTHER CRAFT TITLES

THE MINIATURE WORLD OF PRESSED FLOWERS
by Nona Pettersen

The miniature scale is ideal for the aspiring creating flower arranger, and a stimulating one for those familiar with the usual range of flowers and composition. This attractive, enthusiastic book also explores the plentiful source of plant life, suitable for miniature work, that is surprisingly available in urban areas.

MADE TO TREASURE
Embroideries for all Occasions
edited by Kit Pyman.

This book offers a rich variety of ideas for embroideries to be made to commemorate special occasions – christenings, weddings, birthdays – from simple greetings cards to a gold-work panel for a golden wedding. A heart warming present precisely because it is specially made.

THE SPLENDID SOFT TOY BOOK

The Splendid Soft Toy Book contains a wealth of ideas and pictures for making a wide variety of toys and dolls, from a green corduroy crocodile to detailed traditional, even collectors' dolls. More than 60 full colour pictures and over 70 black and white illustrations show the reader how to fashion appealing figures and animals of all shapes and sizes.
Cased and paperback.

THE CHRISTMAS CRAFTS BOOK

Creative ideas and designs for the whole family to make objects with a Christmas flavour: table and room decorations, stars, Christmas tree ornaments, candles and candlesticks, angels, nativity scenes, paper chains and Christmas cards.

EVERY KIND OF PATCHWORK
edited by Kit Pyman

'Really lives up to its title, and is sufficiently easy to follow that even the most helpless needleperson would be tempted to have a go. But there's plenty, too, for the experienced. *The Guardian.*
Cased and Paperback.

EVERY KIND OF SMOCKING
edited by Kit Pyman

The description of the basic technique is followed by sections on children's clothes, fashion smocking, experimental smocking and creative ideas for finishing touches.

HOW TO MAKE BEAUTIFUL FLOWERS
edited by Valerie Jackson

How to make flowers from all sorts of materials; silk, paper, shells, bread dough, feathers, seeds. The instructions are simple, the materials inexpensive and easy to obtain.

HAVE YOU ANY WOOL?
by Jan Messent

Have You any Wool? is a knitting and crochet book with a difference —which Jan Messent suggests by her challenging sub-title *The creative use of yarn.* She has two principal aims— first to describe the learning of how to knit and crochet in an imaginative way. 'How many of us', she asks, 'can remember the frustrations of having to do it right?' Second, she offers ways in which both experienced and less accomplished knitters and crocheters can extend the boundaries of their work.

If you are interested in any of the above books or any of the art and craft titles published by Search Press and Pitman Publishing Pty Ltd. please send for free catalogue to: Search Press Ltd., Dept B, Wellwood, North Farm Road, Tunbridge Wells, Kent. TN2 3DR, or Pitman Publishing Pty Ltd., Kings Gardens, 95 Coventry Street, South Melbourne, Victoria 3205, Australia.